THE COMPLETE
KETO DIET
COOKBOOK FOR BEGINNERS

Your Easiest Guide to Living the Keto Lifestyle for Lose Weight and Improve Health

8-WEEK MEAL PLAN

MARIANNA HENRY

AMABOOKS
2024

TABLE OF CONTENTS

WHAT IS THE KETO DIET?   6

ADAPT TO KETO IN 8- WEEKS   14

BREAKFAST   25

APPETIZERS AND SNACKS 33

SOUPS AND SALADS 41

FISH AND SEAFOOD 49

POULTRY 57

MEATS 63

VEGGIES 71

EMBRACING YOUR KETO JOURNEY 77

Chapter 1.
What is the Keto Diet?

The Rise and Benefits of the Keto Diet

The keto or ketogenic diet has emerged as one of the most popular and widely discussed nutritional strategies in recent years. Its primary principle involves drastically reducing carbohydrate intake and increasing fat consumption, which pushes the body into a metabolic state known as ketosis. In this state, the body shifts from using glucose (derived from carbs) as its primary energy source to using fat.

The growing popularity of the keto diet stems from its proven effectiveness, not only for weight loss but also for improving metabolic health, managing blood sugar levels, and even enhancing brain function. Many people adopt this eating style as a long-term strategy rather than just a short-term diet.

How the Keto Diet Stands Out from Other Plans

What sets the keto diet apart from other dietary plans is its focus on drastically limiting carbohydrates and significantly increasing fats instead of merely counting calories or following a balanced diet. This shift allows the body to change its energy source and maintain stable blood sugar levels, making the diet appealing for those with type 2 diabetes or insulin resistance.

More people are choosing the keto diet due to its long-term benefits, which include sustained weight loss, improved energy levels, and reduced inflammation. Adopting the keto lifestyle requires discipline, but for many, it proves to be a sustainable and practical approach to maintaining health.

Overview of the Keto Diet

What is Ketosis

Ketosis is a metabolic state where the body shifts from using carbohydrates to fats as the primary energy source. Usually, the body relies on glucose from carbs for fuel, but glucose levels drop when carb intake is significantly reduced. In response, the liver breaks down fats into ketones, the primary energy fuel. This shift occurs when insulin levels decrease, allowing the liver to produce ketones. These ketones are used by the brain, muscles, and other tissues, helping to maintain stable blood sugar levels and avoid the energy fluctuations familiar with high-carb diets.

How the Body Uses Ketones Instead of Glucose

Once in ketosis, the body uses ketones as its primary fuel instead of glucose, providing stable energy for the brain and muscles, especially when low carbs. The brain, which usually depends on glucose, quickly adjusts to ketones, maintaining focus and mental clarity.

Muscles also efficiently use ketones, boosting endurance and performance on the keto diet.

This explains why many on the keto diet experience steady energy and fewer mood swings compared to high-carb diets.

Basics of Keto Nutrition

The keto diet is a low-carb, high-fat approach that shifts the body into ketosis, where fats become the primary fuel. Unlike typical diets focused on carbs, the keto diet limits them to 5-10% of daily intake, while fats make up 70-80% and proteins 20-25%. This shift not only aids weight loss but also helps improve energy levels, stabilize blood sugar, and support overall metabolic health.

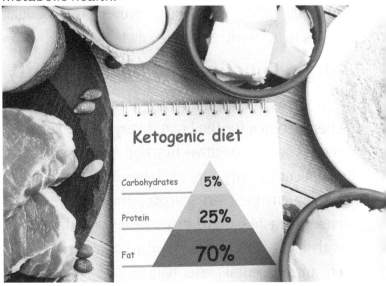

What is the Keto Diet Used For?

Goals and Benefits

Weight Loss

The keto diet is highly effective for weight loss by triggering ketosis, where the body burns fat for energy. A significant benefit is that it burns fat while maintaining muscle mass, which is essential for those looking to lose weight without sacrificing strength. The high-fat content also helps control appetite, reduces snacking, and promotes steady weight loss.

Improvement of Metabolic Health

The keto diet has a strong positive effect on metabolic health. It helps regulate blood sugar levels, vital for people with type 2 diabetes or insulin resistance. Lowering carb intake reduces insulin levels, improving insulin sensitivity and reducing inflammation. This supports overall metabolic balance and helps prevent blood sugar spikes familiar with high-carb diets.

Brain Function and Mental Clarity

Ketones produced during ketosis are a great energy source for the brain. Many on the keto diet report better cognitive function, increased focus, and mental clarity. Since ketones offer more stable, lasting energy than glucose, they help prevent energy crashes and fatigue often linked to high-carb diets. This makes keto a popular choice for enhancing mental performance.

Chronic Disease Management

The keto diet has been effective in managing chronic conditions like type 2 diabetes, epilepsy, and metabolic disorders. Studies show keto can reduce epileptic seizures, especially in children. It also helps regulate blood sugar and lower insulin levels, making it helpful in managing type 2 diabetes. Incorporating keto into treatment plans can improve quality of life and reduce symptoms of these conditions.

Long-term Health Benefits

The keto diet provides long-term benefits for overall health. It reduces inflammation, lowering the risk of chronic diseases like heart disease and diabetes. Keto also promotes stable energy and improves well-being. Adopting a keto lifestyle supports weight management and strengthens the body, making it more resilient to external factors.

Who is the Keto Diet Suitable For?

Ideal Audience for Keto

People looking to manage their weight

The keto diet is perfect for those wanting to control or lose weight. Triggered ketosis helps burn fat while preserving muscle, making it an excellent option for weight loss without sacrificing strength or muscle tone.

Those aiming to improve metabolic health or with insulin resistance

The keto diet helps stabilize blood sugar, making it suitable for those with insulin resistance or type 2 diabetes. Lowering carb intake reduces insulin levels, improves metabolic health, and decreases inflammation.

Individuals seeking enhanced cognitive function

Ketones, the primary energy source of keto, boost brain function. People looking to improve focus, memory, and mental clarity may benefit from the stable, lasting energy provided by the keto diet.

Athletes and fitness enthusiasts aiming to boost endurance

The keto diet supports endurance by using fat as the primary fuel, helping athletes perform longer. Those involved in endurance sports can experience improved performance with keto.

Who May Not Benefit from Keto

The keto diet may not be suitable for those with certain medical conditions, such as chronic liver or kidney disease, as it can place extra strain on the body. Individuals with these conditions should consult a doctor before starting keto.

Additionally, keto may not be ideal for people who prefer a more balanced or flexible diet. The strict carb restriction and the need to closely monitor macronutrients can be challenging for some.

Preparing to Transition to the Keto Diet

Key Preparation Steps Learning the Basics

Before starting the keto diet, it's essential to understand how it works. Learn about macronutrients and their role in ketosis. Keto requires a specific balance: low carbs, high fats, and moderate protein. Knowing these basics will help you follow the diet correctly and avoid common pitfalls.

Meal Planning

Meal planning is critical to keto success. Create a weekly menu that follows keto principles. Prepare meals in advance and keep keto-friendly snacks on hand to avoid accidental carb consumption. This saves time and reduces stress, helping you focus on your diet goals.

Gradual Transition to Keto

To avoid the "keto flu" when starting keto, it's best to reduce carbs gradually. Sudden carb cuts can cause fatigue, headaches, and irritability.

Slowly lowering carbs allows your body to adjust, making the transition to ketosis smoother and with fewer side effects.

Kitchen Cleanout

Starting keto successfully means removing high-carb foods like sugar, bread, pasta, rice, and sweets from your kitchen. This reduces temptation and helps you stay on track. Replace them with keto-friendly options like oils, nuts, fatty meats, low-carb veggies, and healthy fats.

Buying Keto-Friendly Foods

Next, stock up on foods that fit your keto diet. Make a list of healthy fats like avocados, olive oil, coconut oil, and nuts. Include proteins like meat, fish, eggs, and low-carb veggies like greens, broccoli, and zucchini. This ensures you have the right ingredients for balanced keto meals.

What Does Life in Keto Style Entail?

Physical Activity

Moderate physical activity supports ketosis and boosts keto diet results. Strength training, walking, swimming, or yoga can help maintain body tone and promote fat burning. Adjust activity levels to your energy needs, especially in the early stages, to prevent fatigue.

Diet Regimen

Keto relies on a strict macronutrient balance, with fats as the primary energy source. To maintain ketosis, fats should comprise 70-80% of daily intake, 20-25% proteins, and carbs limited to 5-10% (about 20-50 grams daily). Too much protein can be converted into glucose, which may interrupt ketosis. This approach helps the body burn fat for fuel and stabilizes blood sugar and energy levels. Adhering to this macronutrient ratio is essential for keto success.

Long-term Diet Maintenance

Proper meal planning and tracking of macronutrients can help maintain the keto diet long-term. For best results, vary your diet with different fats, proteins, and low-carb vegetables. This prevents nutrient deficiencies and keeps you motivated on your healthy lifestyle journey.

Examples of Foods to Include

For a proper keto diet, focus on foods rich in fats. Include:

- .Fatty Fish: Salmon, mackerel, sardines—high in omega-3s.
- Oils: Olive, coconut, avocado oil.
- Nuts and Seeds: Almonds, walnuts, flaxseeds, chia seeds.
- Avocados: A top source of healthy fats and fiber.
- Meat: Fatty cuts of beef, pork, lamb, and poultry.
- Eggs: An outstanding balance of protein and fat.
- Dairy: Full-fat cheese, butter, heavy cream.

Examples of Foods to Avoid

On keto, avoid high-carb foods that disrupt ketosis, such as:

- Sugar and Sweets: Chocolate, candy, cakes, ice cream.
- Baked Goods: Bread, cookies, pastries.
- Grains: Pasta, rice, oatmeal, quinoa.
- Starchy Vegetables: Potatoes, corn, carrots.
- High-Sugar Fruits: Bananas, grapes, mangoes.

10 Keto Diet Hacks for Beginners

1 Drink More Water
The keto diet can cause dehydration due to water loss. Drink 2-3 liters of water daily to stay hydrated and prevent headaches and fatigue.

2 Add Salt to Your Diet
The keto diet can cause dehydration due to water loss. Drink 2-3 liters of water daily to stay hydrated and prevent headaches and fatigue.

3 Use High-Fat Snacks
Opt for high-fat snacks like nuts, cheese, or avocados when hungry between meals. These help you stay full longer and curb hunger.

4 Transition to Keto Gradually
Gradually reduce carbs to avoid "keto flu" symptoms like energy drops. Cut carbs by 20-30% weekly until reaching the desired intake.

5 Prepare Meals in Advance
Meal prepping ensures you stick to your diet. Having ready-made keto meals helps you avoid non-compliant foods and keeps you on track.

6 Read Product Labels
Check labels to avoid hidden carbs in foods like sauces or packaged meals that might disrupt ketosis.

7 Macronutrient Tracking Apps
Use apps like MyFitnessPal to monitor your carb, fat, and protein intake to follow the correct ratios, especially when starting keto.

8 Try Intermittent Fasting
Adopting a 16/8 fasting schedule can help speed up ketosis and improve appetite control, enhancing your keto results.

9 Keep Variety in Your Diet
Incorporate different fats, proteins, and vegetables into your diet to avoid boredom. Experiment with new recipes to keep meals exciting.

10 Be Patient
Adjusting to ketosis takes time, and "keto flu" symptoms are typical. Patience and adherence to the diet will lead to long-term success.

4 Inadequate Electrolytes

Keto causes water loss, leading to sodium, potassium, and magnesium drops. This can cause headaches and cramps. Increase salt and consider magnesium and potassium supplements.

5 Not Drinking Enough Water

Water loss is expected on keto, which can cause dehydration. Drink at least 2-3 liters daily to stay hydrated and maintain well-being.

6 Not Planning Meals

Lack of planning leads to diet mistakes. Prepare meals in advance to avoid slip-ups and stay on track with your keto goals.

7 Misunderstanding Product Labels

Beginners may need to catch up on hidden carbs in packaged foods. Always read labels carefully to avoid disrupting ketosis.

8 Giving Up Too Soon

Many expect fast results on keto, but progress can take time as the body adapts. Patience and persistence are essential for success.

9 Being Too Strict

Overly rigid restrictions can lead to burnout. Flexibility is essential to make the diet sustainable and enjoyable over time.

10 Ignoring Physical Activity

Focusing only on diet and neglecting exercise can limit results. Moderate activity like walking or strength training boosts metabolism and enhances the benefits of keto.

1 Not Reducing Carbs Enough

Beginners often underestimate food's carbohydrates, including hidden carbohydrates in sauces, processed items, and dairy. This can block ketosis. Always read labels and track carbohydrates accurately to stay within limits.

2 Consuming Too Much Protein

Too much protein can be converted into glucose, disrupting ketosis. Protein should be about 20-25% of your intake to avoid slowing fat loss.

3 Not Enough Fat

Some fear fats and eat too little, but fats are the primary energy source of keto. Lack of fat can cause fatigue. Include healthy fats like avocados, olive oil, and fatty fish.

10 Common Mistakes Beginners Make

Chapter 2.
Adapt to Keto in 8- Weeks

Adapting to the Keto Lifestyle:
A Long-Term Commitment

Transitioning to the keto lifestyle involves more than just dietary changes—it's a comprehensive shift in how your body fuels itself. The process begins by removing high-carb foods from your kitchen and replacing them with keto-friendly options. Creating a well-balanced menu rich in healthy fats, moderate proteins, and low carbohydrates is essential for meeting your daily nutritional needs. This lifestyle focuses on maintaining a daily calorie range of 1800-2000 kcal which supports long-term success in weight management, energy stabilization, and overall well-being.

Keto is more than a short-term diet; it's a sustainable approach that requires discipline and consistency. As your body shifts from relying on glucose to burning fat for energy, you'll experience significant changes in energy levels and cognitive function. However, this transition takes time, and the first eight weeks are crucial for laying the foundation for a successful keto journey.

The First Four Weeks: Adapting Your Body to Keto

The initial four weeks of the keto diet are about adapting your body to its new energy source—fat. During this time, your body gradually switches from using glucose to ketones for fuel. Following a meal plan with three meals per day is recommended, as well as maintaining a daily intake of 1800-2000 kcal to support your body through this adaptation period. You might begin to notice increased mental clarity, steady energy levels, and improved well-being as your body enters ketosis. This is a critical phase in which you allow your metabolism to adapt smoothly and efficiently to the fat-burning process.

Weeks 4-8: Transitioning to Two Meals a Day and Intermittent Fasting

After your body has adjusted to the keto diet, the next step is to transition to two meals a day while keeping your daily calorie intake at 1800-2000 kcal. This phase introduces intermittent fasting with a 16/8 schedule, where you fast for 16 hours and consume food during an 8-hour window. This method enhances fat burning and helps maintain ketosis more efficiently. Intermittent fasting has been shown to improve appetite control, boost metabolism, and increase energy, making it a powerful tool for long-term success in keto.

During weeks 4-8, the goal is to deepen the state of ketosis and become more accustomed to a sustainable eating routine. This period helps solidify the keto lifestyle as part of your daily routine, allowing you to fully embrace the benefits of fat-burning for energy.

Key Steps for the First 4 Weeks:

- Remove high-carb foods and stock up on keto-friendly ingredients.
- Follow a three-meal-a-day plan to maintain energy and nutrient balance.
- Give your body time to adjust to using fat as its primary energy source, leading to a smooth transition into ketosis.

Key Insights for Weeks 4-8:

- Transition to two meals per day while maintaining your daily calorie intake.
- Incorporate intermittent fasting (16/8) to optimize fat burning and improve metabolism.
- Continue experiencing enhanced energy, mental clarity, and overall well-being as ketosis strengthens

Shopping List

for Weeks 1 and 3

Fish and Seafood

- Alaskan pollock fillets - 2 (6 ounces each)
- Tilapia fillets - 2 (6 ounces each)
- Tuna steaks - 2 (6 ounces each)
- Salmon smoked - 8 ounces
- Salmon fillets - 10 ounces
- Salmon salted - 4 ounces
- Shrimp medium - 35

Meat

- Bacon - 4 slices
- Chicken fillets - 4(6 ounces each)
- Chicken breasts - 3 pounds
- Chicken ground - 1 pounds
- Turkey ground - 1 pounds
- Pork tenderloin - 1 pounds
- Ground beef or pork - 2 pounds

Vegetables

- Asparagus - 2 bunch
- Arugula fresh - 5 cups
- Broccoli florets - 4 cups
- Basil leaves fresh - 4 tablespoon
- Bell peppers - 2
- Cauliflower - 2
- Cauliflower florets - 4 cups
- Cucumber - 3
- Dill Fresh - 2 tablespoon
- Garlic cloves - 20
- Ginger, minced - 1 teaspoon
- Mushrooms, sliced - 3 cups
- Onion small - 3
- Onion red - 1
- Parsley Fresh - 8 tablespoon
- Radishes - 4
- Red bell pepper - 2
- Parsley fresh - 8 tablespoon
- Mixed Greens (spinach, arugula, etc.) - 5 cup
- Tomatoes Cherry, sliced - 4 cup
- Tomatoes small, sliced -1+1/2 cup
- Zucchini medium - 3

Pantry Items

- Basil dried - 1 teaspoon
- Baking powder
- Black pepper, freshly ground
- Chia seeds - 1/2 cup
- Cinnamon , ground - 1 teaspoon
- Coffee
- Flour hazelnut - 1/2 cup
- Flour cashew - 1/4 cup
- Flour almond - 1+3/4 cup
- Garlic powder - 8 teaspoon
- Onion powder - 2 teaspoon
- Olives - 8
- Oregano dried - 4 teaspoon
- Paprika - 3 teaspoon
- Seeds mixed (sunflower, pumpkin, sesame) - 5 tablespoon
- Sweetener (like stevia) - 4 teaspoon
- Thyme dried - 2 teaspoon
- Vanilla extract - 1/2 teaspoon
- Walnuts - 1/4 cup

Fruits

- Avocados - 8
- Fresh mixed berries (strawberries, raspberries, blueberries) - 1 cup
- lemons - 3

Canned and Bottled Items

- Apple cider vinegar - 2 teaspoon
- Coconut oil - 14 tablespoon
- Chicken broth - 10 cup
- Mustard Dijon - 5 tablespoon
- Mustard whole-grain - 1 tablespoon
- MCT coconut oil - 1 tablespoon
- Mayonnaise - 1/2 cup
- Olive oil - 28 tablespoon
- Pesto sauce - 1/2 cup
- Tuna in olive oil - 1 can

Eggs, Dairy and Dairy Alternatives

- Almond milk - 2 + 1/2 cup
- Butter - 1+1/2 cup
- Cheese cream - 1/4 cup
- Cheddar cheese - 1+1/4 cup
- Coconut cream - 1/4 cup
- Eggs Quail - 8
- Eggs large - 34
- Feta cheese - 1/4 cup
- Heavy cream - 5 cup
- Mascarpone cheese - 3/4 cup
- Ricotta cheese - 1/2 cup
- Parmesan cheese (grated) - 2 1/2 cup

Meal Plan for Weeks 1 and 3

	Beakfasts	Lunch		Dinner

Sunday

Bulletproof Coffee p.35
Shrimp, Soft Fried Egg, Avocado p.26

Salad of Tomatoes, Avocado and Arugula p.42

Baked Salmon with Asparagus p.50

Beef Tenderloin p.67

Calories: 1960/ Fats: 165g/ Protein: 88g/Net Carbs: 17g

Monday

Vegetarian Smoothie p.36
Salted Salmon Salad with Greens, Cucumbers p.27

Cauliflower Cream Soup with Bacon p.43

Chicken Breasts with Pesto Sauce p.59

Casserole with Salmon . 54

Calories: 1900/ Fats: 153g/ Protein: 100g/Net Carbs: 20g

Tuesday

Chia Seed Pudding p.32
Broccoli and Zucchini Fritters p.27

Broccoli Cream Soup with Cream and Parmesan p.43

Stir Fry with Chicken and Asparagus p.61

Grilled Tuna Steak p. 52

Calories: 1790/ Fats: 132g/ Protein: 98g/Net Carbs: 20g

Wednesday

Bulletproof Coffee p.35
Avocado Toast with Smoked Salmon, Scrambled Eggs p.28

Keto Turkey Meatball Soup with Zucchini Noodles and Carrot p.44

Fried Tilapia Fish Fillet with Avocado and Vegetables p.55

Chicken Fillet Stuffed with Cheese p.62

Calories: 1850/ Fats: 147g/ Protein: 107g/Net Carbs: 18g

Thursday

Spinach Pancakes with Salmon, Grilled Bell Pepper p.29

Salad of Fresh Vegetables, Grilled Shrimp, and Quail Eggs p.45

Chicken Meatballs with Tomatoes p.58

Creamed Spinach p.72
White Fish Alaskan Pollock p.55

Calories: 1810/ Fats: 144g/ Protein: 108g/Net Carbs: 16g

Friday

Keto Almond Flour Crepes p.39

Cream of Mushroom Soup p.45

Tuna Salad with Cherry Tomatoes and Greens p.47

Stuffed Bell Peppers with Meat p.70

Calories: 1720/ Fats: 139g/ Protein: 81g/Net Carbs: 24g

Saturday

Bulletproof Coffee p.35
Omelet Pulyar with Shrimp and Grilled Mushrooms p.30

Shrimp with Garlic and Dill p.51

Avocado Eggs Salad p.48

Cauliflower Rice p.75
Meatballs in Creamy Parmesan Sauce p.69

Calories: 1770/ Fats: 156g/ Protein: 90g/Net Carbs: 15g

Shopping List
for Weeks 2 and 4

Fish and Seafood

- Cod fillets - 2 (6 ounces each)
- Sea bass fillets - 4 (6 ounces each)
- Salmon smoked - 4 ounces
- Shrimp medium - 40
- Tilapia fillets - 2 (6 ounces each)
- Tuna steaks - 2 (6 ounces each)

Meat

- Bacon - 4 slices
- Chicken fillets - 2 (6 ounces each)
- Chicken breasts - 4 pounds
- Ground beef or pork - 2 pounds
- lamb chops - 4 (6 ounces each)
- Pork spare ribs - 2 pounds
- Pork tenderloin - 1 pounds
- Ribeye steaks - 2 (8 ounces each)
- Turkey ground - 2 pounds

Vegetables

- Asparagus - 3 bunch
- Arugula fresh - 2 cups
- Broccoli florets - 1 cups
- Basil leaves fresh - 4 tablespoon
- Bell peppers - 2
- Fresh green beans, trimmed - 8 oz
- Cabbage, chopped - 1/2 head
- Cauliflower rice - 1 cup
- Cauliflower florets - 3 cups
- Cucumber - 2
- Coriander fresh - 1/4 cup
- Dill Fresh - 2 tablespoon
- Garlic cloves - 24
- Ginger, minced - 1 teaspoon
- Microgreens - 1 cups
- Mixed Greens (spinach, arugula, etc.) - 2 cup
- Mushrooms, sliced - 3 cups
- Mixed Greens (spinach, arugula, etc.) - 7 cup
- Onion small , red- 5
- Parsley Fresh - 12 tablespoon
- Radishes - 4
- Red bell pepper - 1
- Parsley fresh - 8 tablespoon
- Tomatoes small,Cherry, sliced - 5 cup
- Zucchini medium - 4

Pantry Items

- Basil dried - 1 teaspoon
- Baking powder -3 teaspoon
- Black pepper, freshly ground
- Chia seeds - 1/2 cup
- Cocoa powder -1/4 cup
- Coffee
- Flour hazelnut, cashew -1+1/4 cup
- Flour almond - 1+3/4 cup
- Garlic,Onion powder - 10 teaspoon
- Olives - 8
- Oregano dried - 4 teaspoon
- Paprika - 3 teaspoon
- Seeds mixed (sunflower, pumpkin, sesame) - 5 tablespoon
- Sweetener (like stevia) - 4 teaspoon
- Vanilla extract - 1/2 teaspoon
- Walnuts - 1/4 cup

Fruits

- Avocados - 5
- Fresh mixed berries (strawberries, raspberries, blueberries) - 1 cup
- lemons - 3

Canned and Bottled Items

- Apple cider vinegar - 6 teaspoon
- Coconut oil - 22 tablespoon
- Chicken broth - 7 cup
- Mustard Dijon,whole-grain - 3 tablespoon
- MCT coconut oil - 3 tablespoon
- Olive oil - 36 tablespoon
- Pesto sauce - 1/4 cup
- Tuna in olive oil - 1 can

Eggs, Dairy and Dairy Alternatives

- Almond milk - 1 cup
- Butter - 2+1/2 cup
- Cheese, coconut cream - 1/2
- Cheddar cheese - 1+1/4 cup
- Eggs Quail - 4
- Eggs large - 18
- Feta cheese - 3/4 cup
- Greek yogurt (full-fat) - 1 cup
- Heavy cream - 5 cup
- Mozzarella,Ricotta cheese -2cup
- Parmesan cheese (grated) - 3 cup

Meal Plan

	Beakfasts	Lunch		Dinner
Sunday	Ketogenic Fudge Brownie p.38 / Roll of Scrambled Eggs with Cauliflower, Cheese p.31	Ground Beef Cabbage Soup p.48	Baked Seabass p. 53	Roasted Lamb Chops p.65

Calories: 1780/ Fats: 140g/ Protein: 97g/Net Carbs: 14g

Monday	Bulletproof Coffee p.35 / Shrimp, Soft Fried Egg, Avocado p.26	Baked Atlantic Salmon p.53	Greek Salad p.46	Ribeye Steak p.64

Calories: 1870/ Fats: 156g/ Protein: 93g/Net Carbs: 14g

Tuesday	Spinach Pancakes with Salmon, Grilled Bell Pepper p.29	Chicken Breast Salad with Zucchini, Cherry Tomatoes, p.46	Shrimp with Garlic and Dill p.51	Braised Pork Spare Ribs, p.66

Calories: 1860/ Fats: 136g/ Protein: 97g/Net Carbs: 18g

Wednesday	Keto Greek Yogurt with Nuts p.32 / Omelet Pulyar with Shrimp and Grilled Mushrooms p.30	Grilled Tuna Steak with Pepper and Avocado Cucumber Salsa p. 52	Cream of Mushroom Soup p. 45	Turkey Meatloaf Roll p.60

Calories: 1720/ Fats: 136g/ Protein: 85g/Net Carbs: 19g

Thursday	Chia Seed Pudding with Milk p.32 / Broccoli and Zucchini Fritters p.27	Chicken Breast Roll with Bacon, Cheese, and Dill, p.62	Tuna Salad with Cherry Tomatoes and Greens p.47	Zucchini Pasta Topped p.76 / Cod Fillet with Garlic Butter Sauce p.56

Calories: 2000/ Fats: 160g/ Protein: 104g/Net Carbs: 20g

Friday	Bulletproof Coffee, p.35 / Spinach Pancakes with Chicken and Salad p.29	Meatballs in Creamy Parmesan Sauce p.69	Cauliflower Puree with Cream p.76	Green Asparagus p.75 / Chicken Fillet Stuffed with Cheese p.62

Calories: 1950/ Fats: 167g/ Protein: 92g/Net Carbs: 17g

Saturday	Bulletproof Coffee p.35 / Avocado and Quail Egg Toasts p.35	Pork Tenderloin with Mustard Sauce p.67	Garlicky Green Beans p.73	Cauliflower Rice p.75 / Grilled Turkey Breast with Avocado p.60

Calories: 1720/ Fats: 144g/ Protein: 87g/Net Carbs: 17g

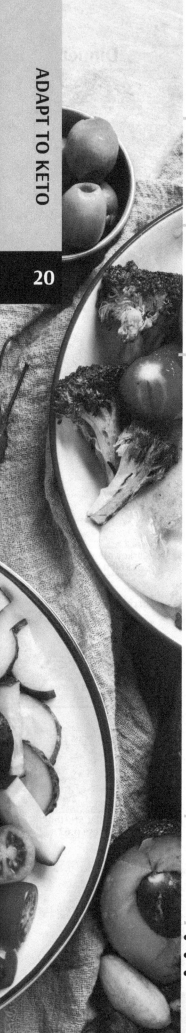

Shopping List
for Weeks 5 and 7

Fish and Seafood

- Salmon fillets - 3 (6 ounces each)
- Salmon smoked - 4 ounces
- Sea bass fillets - 2 (6 ounces each)
- Shrimp medium - 32
- Tuna steaks - 2 (6 ounces each)

Meat

- Bacon - 6 slices
- Chicken - 2 fillets (6 ounces each)
- Chicken breasts - 1 pounds
- Pork spare ribs - 2 pounds
- Pork tenderloin - 1 pounds
- Ground beef or pork - 2 pounds

Vegetables

- Asparagus - 1 bunch
- Arugula fresh - 3 cups
- Broccoli florets - 4 cups
- Basil leaves fresh - 4 tablespoon
- Bell peppers - 2
- Cauliflower - 2
- Cauliflower florets - 4 cups
- Cucumber - 3
- Dill Fresh - 2 tablespoon
- Garlic cloves - 20
- Ginger, minced - 1 teaspoon
- Mushrooms, sliced - 3 cups
- Lettuce
- Onion small - 3
- Onion red - 1
- Parsley Fresh - 8 tablespoon
- Radishes - 4
- Red bell pepper - 2
- Parsley fresh - 8 tablespoon
- Mixed Greens (spinach, arugula, etc.) - 5 cup
- Tomatoes Cherry, sliced - 4 cup
- Tomatoes small, sliced -1+1/2 cup
- Zucchini medium - 5

Fruits

- Avocados - 6
- Fresh mixed berries (strawberries, raspberries, blueberries) - 1 cup
- lemons - 3

Pantry Items

- Basil dried - 1 teaspoon
- Baking powder
- Black pepper, freshly ground
- Coffee
- Chia seeds - 1/2 cup
- Cinnamon , ground - 1 teaspoon
- Flour hazelnut - 1/2 cup
- Flour cashew - 1/4 cup
- Flour almond - 1+3/4 cup
- Garlic powder - 8 teaspoon
- Onion powder - 2 teaspoon
- Olives - 8
- Oregano dried - 4 teaspoon
- Paprika - 3 teaspoon
- Seeds mixed (sunflower, pumpkin, sesame) - 5 tablespoon
- Sweetener (like stevia) - 4 teaspoon
- Thyme dried - 2 teaspoon
- Vanilla extract - 1/2 teaspoon
- Walnuts - 1/4 cup

Canned and Bottled Items

- Apple cider vinegar - 5 teaspoon
- Coconut oil - 14 tablespoon
- Chicken broth - 10 cup
- Mustard Dijon - 5 tablespoon
- Mustard whole-grain - 1 tablespoon
- MCT coconut oil - 1 tablespoon
- Mayonnaise - 1/2 cup
- Olive oil - 28 tablespoon
- Pesto sauce - 1/2 cup
- Tuna in olive oil - 1 can

Eggs, Dairy and Dairy Alternatives

- Almond milk - 2 + 1/2 cup
- Butter - 1+1/2 cup
- Cheese cream - 1/4 cup
- Cheddar cheese (shredded) - 1+1/4 cup
- Coconut cream - 1/4 cup
- Eggs Quail - 8
- Eggs large - 34
- Feta cheese - 1/4 cup
- Heavy cream - 5 cup
- Mascarpone cheese - 3/4 cup
- Ricotta cheese - 1/2 cup
- Parmesan cheese (grated) - 2 1/2 cup

Meta Plan for Weeks 5 and 7

Lunch

ADAPT TO KETO

Sunday

Bulletproof Coffee p.35
Roll of Scrambled Eggs with Cauliflower, Cheese p.31

Ketogenic Fudge Brownie p.38

Baked Broccoli p.74
Ground Beef Cabbage Soup p.48

Dinner

Baked Seabass p.53

Calories: 1780/ Fats: 138g/ Protein: 71g/Net Carbs: 17g

Monday

Bulletproof Coffee p.35
Shrimp, Soft Fried Egg, Avocado p.26

Chia Seed Pudding with Almond Milk p.32

Cauliflower Rice p.75
Greek Salad p.46

Baked Atlantic Salmon p.53

Calories: 1770/ Fats: 160g/ Protein: 66g/Net Carbs: 16g

Tuesday

Bulletproof Coffee p.35
Casserole with Salmon and Broccoli p.54

Keto Nuts-Chocolate Fat Bombs p.37

Chicken Breast Salad with Zucchini p.46

Zucchini Stir-Fried p.73
Braised Pork Spare Ribs p.66

Calories: 1860/ Fats: 146g/ Protein: 79g/Net Carbs: 16g

Wednesday

Keto Greek Yogurt with Nuts p.32
Omelet Pulyar with Shrimp and Grilled Mushrooms p.30

Keto Almond Flour Crepes p.39

Cream of Mushroom Soup p. 45

Cauliflower Puree p.78
Grilled Tuna Steak with Pepper and Salsa p.52

Calories: 1700/ Fats: 141g/ Protein: 65g/Net Carbs: 22g

Thursday

Bulletproof Coffee, p.35
Broccoli and Zucchini Fritters p.27

Chicken Breast Roll with Bacon, Cheese, and Dill, p.62

Tuna Salad with Cherry Tomatoes and Greens p.47

Zucchini Pasta p.76
Chicken Breast Roll with Bacon, Cheese, p.62

Calories: 1870/ Fats: 154g/ Protein: 82g/Net Carbs: 19g

Friday

Bulletproof Coffee p.35
Spinach Pancakes with Chicken and Salad p.29

Keto Fat Bombs with Coconut p.37

Meatballs in Creamy Parmesan Sauce p.69

Avocado Eggs Salad p.50
Green Asparagus with Hollandaise Sauce p.75

Calories: 1820/ Fats: 164g/ Protein: 63g/Net Carbs: 13g

Saturday

Bulletproof Coffee p.35
Salad of Fresh Vegetables, Grilled Shrimp, and Quail Eggs p.45

Avocado and Quail Egg Toasts p.35

Pork Tenderloin with Mustard Sauce p.67

Pumpkin Spice-Cacao Bombs p.38
Cauliflower Puree with Cream p.76

Calories: 1770/ Fats: 154g/ Protein: 53g/Net Carbs: 18g

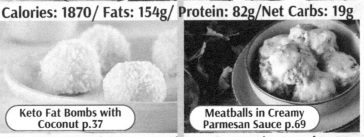

Shopping List
for Weeks 6 and 8

Fish and Seafood

- Alaskan pollock fillets - 2 (6 ounces each)
- Tuna steaks -2 (6 oz each)
- Salmon smoked - 8 ounces
- Salmon fillets - 3 (6 ounces each)
- Salmon salted - 4 ounces
- Shrimp medium - 28

Meat

- Chicken - 2 fillets (6 ounces each)
- Chicken breasts - 2 pounds
- Chicken ground - 1 pounds
- Turkey ground - 1 pounds
- Turkey breast - 1 pounds
- Ground beef or pork - 2 pounds

Vegetables

- Asparagus - 1 bunch
- Arugula fresh - 5 cups
- Broccoli florets - 4 cups
- Basil leaves fresh - 4 tablespoon
- Bell peppers - 2
- Cauliflower - 2
- Cauliflower florets - 4 cups
- Cucumber - 3
- Dill Fresh - 2 tablespoon
- Garlic cloves - 20
- Ginger, minced - 1 teaspoon
- Mushrooms, sliced - 3 cups
- Onion small - 3
- Onion red - 1
- Parsley Fresh - 8 tablespoon
- Radishes - 4
- Red bell pepper - 2
- Parsley fresh - 8 tablespoon
- Mixed Greens (spinach, arugula, etc.) - 5 cup
- Tomatoes Cherry, sliced - 4 cup
- Tomatoes small, sliced -1+1/2 cup
- Zucchini medium - 3

Pantry Items

- Basil dried - 1 teaspoon
- Baking powder
- Black pepper, freshly ground
- Chia seeds - 1/2 cup
- Cinnamon , ground - 1 teaspoon
- Coffee
- Flour hazelnut - 1/2 cup
- Flour cashew - 1/4 cup
- Flour almond - 1+3/4 cup
- Garlic powder - 8 teaspoon
- Onion powder - 2 teaspoon
- Olives - 8
- Oregano dried - 4 teaspoon
- Paprika - 3 teaspoon
- Seeds mixed (sunflower, pumpkin, sesame) - 5 tablespoon
- Sweetener (like stevia) - 4 teaspoon
- Thyme dried - 2 teaspoon
- Vanilla extract - 1/2 teaspoon
- Walnuts - 1/4 cup

Fruits

- Avocados - 8
- Fresh mixed berries (strawberries, raspberries, blueberries) - 1 cup
- lemons - 3

Canned and Bottled Items

- Apple cider vinegar - 2 teaspoon
- Coconut oil - 14 tablespoon
- Chicken broth - 10 cup
- Mustard Dijon - 5 tablespoon
- Mustard whole-grain - 1 tablespoon
- MCT coconut oil - 1 tablespoon
- Mayonnaise - 1/2 cup
- Olive oil - 28 tablespoon
- Pesto sauce - 1/2 cup
- Tuna in olive oil - 1 can

Eggs, Dairy and Dairy Alternatives

- Almond milk - 2 + 1/2 cup
- Butter - 1+1/2 cup
- Cheese cream - 1/4 cup
- Cheddar cheese (shredded) - 1+1/4 cup
- Coconut cream - 1/4 cup
- Eggs Quail - 8
- Eggs large - 34
- Feta cheese - 1/4 cup
- Heavy cream - 5 cup
- Mascarpone cheese - 3/4 cup
- Ricotta cheese - 1/2 cup
- Parmesan cheese (grated) - 2 1/2 cup

Meal Plan for Weeks 6 and 8

Lunch | Dinner

Sunday

Bulletproof Coffee p.35
Shrimp, Soft Fried Egg, Avocado p.26

Keto Nut Butter p 40

Ketogenic Fudge Brownie p.38
Salad of Tomatoes, Avocado, Arugula, Radish, and Seeds p.42

Baked Salmon p.50

Calories: 1870/ Fats: 162g/ Protein: 77g/Net Carbs: 16g

Monday

Bulletproof Coffee p.35
Salted Salmon Salad with Greens, Cucumbers, Eggs p. 27

Vegetarian Smoothie with Fresh Berries, Avocado p.36

Cauliflower Cream Soup p.43
Chicken Breasts with Pesto Sauce, p.59

Cauliflower Puree p.76

Calories: 1820/ Fats: 152g/ Protein: 176g/Net Carbs: 20g

Tuesday

Bulletproof Coffee p. 35
Chia Seed Pudding with Almond Milk p. 32

Casserole with Salmon and Broccoli p. 54

Greek Salad p. 48
Chicken Breast Salad with Zucchini p.43

Grilled Tuna Steak with Pepper and Salsa p.52

Calories: 1830/ Fats: 143g/ Protein: 80g/Net Carbs: 20g

Wednesday

Bulletproof Coffee p. 35
Avocado Toast with Smoked Salmon, Scrambled Eggs p.28

Keto Nuts-Chocolate Fat Bombs p.37

Keto Turkey Meatball Soup with Zucchini Noodles and Carrot p.44

Tuna Salad p. 47
Chicken Fillet Stuffed p.62

Calories: 1900/ Fats: 152g/ Protein: 112g/Net Carbs: 20g

Thursday

Bulletproof Coffee, p.35
Spinach Pancakes with Salmon, Grilled Bell Pepper p.29

Chia Seed Pudding with Milk p.32

Salad of Fresh Vegetables, Grilled Shrimp, and Quail Eggs p.45

White Fish Alaskan Pollock with Spinach p.55
Creamed Spinach Side Dish with Onion p.72

Calories: 1810/ Fats: 152g/ Protein: 110g/Net Carbs: 14g

Friday

Bulletproof Coffee, p.35
Keto Almond Flour Crepes p.39

Vegetarian Smoothie with Fresh Berries, Avocado p.36

Avocado Eggs Salad p.50
Tuna Salad with Cherry Tomatoes and Greens p.47

Cream of Mushroom Soup p.45
Stuffed Bell Peppers with Minced Meat p.70

Calories: 1720/ Fats: 134g/ Protein: 81g/Net Carbs: 13g

Saturday

Bulletproof Coffee p.35
Omelet Pulyar with Shrimp and Grilled Mushrooms, p.30

Ketogenic Fudge Brownie p.38

Ground Beef Cabbage Soup p.48

Cauliflower Rice p.75
Grilled Turkey Breast with Avocado p.60

Calories: 1770/ Fats: 156g/ Protein: 90g/Net Carbs: 15g

Long-Term Benefits: Sustaining the Keto Lifestyle

By the end of the first eight weeks, you will have set the foundation for a long-term keto lifestyle. The key to sustaining this diet lies in balance, discipline, and flexibility. Regular meal planning and physical activity play important roles in maintaining energy levels, preventing plateaus, and enhancing metabolic health.

As keto becomes a natural part of your routine, you'll likely notice lasting improvements in mental clarity, stable energy, and effective weight management.

his lifestyle allows you to enjoy the benefits of fat-burning for energy while supporting overall health and well-being. The initial transition period may be challenging, but with consistency and patience, keto can offer a sustainable and rewarding approach to healthy living.

Chapter 3
Breakfast

Eggs: A Keto Powerhouse

Eggs are an essential food on the keto diet, providing a perfect balance of protein and healthy fats. Eating 2-3 eggs daily makes it easy to reach your protein goals without adding many carbs.

Eggs are rich in choline, which supports brain health, and contain essential vitamins like B12 and D for energy and immunity. Their high-quality protein keeps you feeling full and helps maintain muscle mass, which is important when losing weight on keto. Quick to prepare and versatile, eggs can be enjoyed in countless keto-friendly recipes, from breakfasts to snacks.

SHRIMP, SOFT FRIED EGG AND AVOCADO

 Excellent   **Easy**   **2 Servings**   **10 min.**   **10 min.**

Ingredients:

- 8 medium shrimp, peeled and deveined
- 2 large eggs
- 1 ripe avocado, sliced
- 1 small tomato, sliced
- 1/4 cup walnuts, chopped
- 6-8 olives

- 2 tablespoons butter
- 1 tablespoon olive oil
- 1/2 teaspoon garlic powder
- Salt and pepper to taste
- 1 tablespoon lemon juice
- Fresh parsley or cilantro for garnish (optional)

Instructions:

1. Heat 1 tablespoon of butter in a skillet over medium heat. Cook the shrimp on each side for 2-3 minutes, seasoning with garlic powder, salt, and pepper. Set aside.
2. In the same skillet, heat the remaining butter and olive oil. Fry the eggs for 3-4 minutes until the whites are set and the yolks remain soft.
3. Drizzle the avocado slices with lemon juice and lightly season with salt.
4. Arrange the shrimp, eggs, avocado, tomato slices, walnuts, and olives on a plate. Garnish with fresh parsley or cilantro if desired.

Per serving:

Calories: 480 | Fats: 38g | Protein: 24g | Carbs: 8g | Net Carbs: 4g | Fiber: 4g
Fat 72% | Protein 23% | Carb 5%

SALTED SALMON SALAD WITH GREENS, CUCUMBERS, EGGS, AND AVOCADO

Ingredients:

- 4 oz salted salmon, sliced
- 2 large eggs, boiled and sliced
- 1 cup mixed greens (spinach, arugula, etc.)
- 1/2 cucumber, sliced
- 1 avocado, halved and flesh scooped out
- 2 tablespoons olive oil
- 1 tablespoon lemon juice
- Salt and pepper to taste

Instructions:

1. Scoop out the avocado flesh, mash it, and season with salt, pepper, and lemon juice.
2. Arrange the mixed greens, cucumber, and boiled eggs on a plate. Add the mashed avocado and top with slices of salted salmon.
3. Drizzle with olive oil, season with more salt and pepper if desired, and garnish with fresh dill.

Per serving:

Calories: 400 | Fats: 32g | Protein: 20g | Carbs: 5g | Net Carbs: 3g | Fiber: 2g
Fat 78% / Protein 20% / Carb 2%

BROCCOLI AND ZUCCHINI FRITTERS

 Excellent   2 Servings

 Easy   10 min. 15 min.

Ingredients:

- 1/2 cup broccoli florets, finely chopped
- 1/2 cup zucchini, grated
- 2 large eggs
- 1/4 cup almond flour
- 1/2 teaspoon paprika
- 2 tablespoons heavy cream
- 1 tablespoon coconut oil (for frying)
- Salt and pepper to taste
- 1/2 teaspoon garlic powder
- 1/2 cup shredded cheddar cheese

Instructions:

1. Combine the chopped broccoli, grated zucchini, eggs, almond flour, cheddar cheese, heavy cream, garlic powder, paprika, salt, and pepper in a large bowl. Mix well until all ingredients are combined.
2. Heat coconut oil in a skillet over medium heat. Scoop 2-3 tablespoons of the fritter mixture into the skillet and flatten slightly.
3. Fry the fritters on each side for 3-4 minutes until golden brown and crispy.
4. Transfer the fritters to a plate and serve immediately.

Per serving:

Calories: 380 | Fats: 28g | Protein: 18g | Carbs: 7g | Net Carbs: 4g | Fiber: 3g
Fat 70% / Protein 24% / Carb 6%

Avocado: A Keto Essential

Including half an avocado daily in your keto diet is a great way to boost nutrient intake. Avocados are rich in healthy fats, fiber, and potassium, helping you stay full longer and keeping energy levels steady—essential for keto success. Select a ripe, soft avocado for the best flavor and absorption.

Adding avocado to meals several times a week aids digestion, supports heart health, and helps you maintain the right fat balance. Its mild taste and creamy texture pair well with many keto dishes, from salads to smoothies.

AVOCADO TOAST WITH SMOKED SALMON, SCRAMBLED EGGS

  Excellent   **Easy**   **2 Servings**   **10 min.**   **10 min.**

Ingredients:

- 2 slices of keto bread (recipe on page 34)
- 1 ripe avocado, sliced
- 4 oz smoked salmon
- 4 large eggs
- 1 cup fresh arugula

- 2 tablespoons heavy cream
- 1 tablespoon butter
- Salt and pepper to taste
- Lemon juice (optional)
- Fresh dill for garnish (optional)

Instructions:

1. Toast the keto bread slices. Slice the avocado and place it on top of the toast—season with salt, pepper, and lemon juice.
2. In a bowl, whisk the eggs with heavy cream, salt, and pepper.
3. Heat butter in a skillet over medium heat and cook the scrambled eggs, stirring gently until soft and creamy.
4. Arrange the plate with avocado toast, scrambled eggs, and smoked salmon. Add a handful of fresh arugula on the side. Garnish with fresh dill if desired.

Per serving:

Calories: 480 | Fats: 40g | Protein: 22g | Carbs: 7g | Net Carbs: 4g | Fiber: 3g
Fat 80% / Protein 18% / Carb 2%

SPINACH PANCAKES WITH SALMON, GRILLED BELL PEPPER, MASCARPONE

Ingredients:

For the Pancakes:
- 2 large eggs
- 1 cup fresh spinach leaves
- 1/4 cup almond flour
- 1/4 cup heavy cream
- 1 tablespoon butter for frying
- Salt and pepper to taste

For the Filling:
- 4 oz smoked salmon
- 1/2 red bell pepper, grilled and sliced
- 1/4 cup mascarpone cheese
- 1 tablespoon pesto

Fresh basil or parsley for garnish

Instructions:

1. Mix spinach, eggs, almond flour, heavy cream, salt, and pepper until smooth in a blender.
2. Heat butter in a skillet over medium heat. Pour batter into small pancakes and cook for 2-3 minutes on each side until cooked. Set aside.
3. Spread mascarpone cheese on each pancake. Top with slices of smoked salmon, grilled bell pepper, and a pesto drizzle.
4. Roll or fold the pancakes in half, garnish with fresh basil or parsley.

Per serving:

Calories: 450 | Fats: 35g | Protein: 20g | Carbs: 6g | Net Carbs: 4g | Fiber: 2g
Fat 77% / Protein 18% / Carb 5%

Excellent
 2 Servings

Medium **15 min.** **10 min.**

SPINACH PANCAKES WITH CHICKEN AND SALAD

Ingredients:

For the Pancakes:
- 2 large eggs
- 1 cup fresh spinach leaves
- 1/4 cup almond flour
- 1/4 cup heavy cream
- 1 tablespoon butter for frying
- Salt and pepper to taste

For the Filling:
- 4 oz cooked chicken breast, sliced
- 1/2 cup mixed salad greens (arugula)
- 1/4 cup cherry tomatoes, halved
- 2 tablespoons olive oil
- 1 tablespoon lemon juice

Instructions:

1. Toss the mixed salad greens, cherry tomatoes, olive oil, lemon juice, salt, and pepper in a bowl.
2. Fill each pancake with slices of chicken and the salad mixture. Roll or fold the pancakes, garnish with parsley or basil, and serve.

Per serving:

Calories: 420 | Fats: 33g | Protein: 24g | Carbs: 5g | Net Carbs: 3g | Fiber: 2g
Fat 76% / Protein 22% / Carb 2%

OMELET PULYAR WITH SHRIMP AND GRILLED MUSHROOMS

Excellent

Medium

2 Servings

10 min.

10 min.

Ingredients:

- 4 large eggs, separated
- 1/4 cup heavy cream
- 3 oz shrimp, cooked and peeled (about 8 small shrimp)
- 2 small mushrooms, sliced
- 1 tablespoon butter

- 1 radish, thinly sliced (for garnish)
- 2 cherry tomatoes, halved (for garnish)
- Salt and pepper to taste

Instructions:

1. Separate egg whites from yolks. Whisk the egg whites until stiff peaks form. In a separate bowl, mix the yolks with heavy cream, salt, and pepper.
2. Heat butter in a skillet over medium heat. Pour in the yolk mixture and cook for 40-45 seconds until the yolk is set. Spread the whipped egg whites over the yolk layer, smooth them, and cover with a lid. Cook on medium heat for 8 minutes.
3. Meanwhile, grill the shrimp and mushroom slices in another skillet over medium heat until golden and cooked through about 5-6 minutes.
4. Once the omelet is fully cooked, remove from the skillet, cut into two portions, and fold each in half. Top with the grilled shrimp and mushrooms, and garnish with radish slices and cherry tomatoes. Serve immediately.

Per serving:

Calories: 350 | Fats: 28g | Protein: 20g | Carbs: 4g | Net Carbs: 2g | Fiber: 2g
Fat 72% / Protein 24% / Carb 4%

ROLL OF SCRAMBLED EGGS WITH CAULIFLOWER, CHEESE, AND SPINACH

Spinach: A Keto-Friendly Nutrient Boost

Spinach is an excellent keto, offering essential nutrients with few carbs. Packed with iron, magnesium, and potassium, it supports muscle function and energy levels, which are key for keto success. Spinach also promotes immune health and is high in antioxidants and vitamins A and C. Adding a cup to your meals daily provides these nutrients without many carbs, making it perfect for salads, smoothies, or as a low-carb side.

 Excellent   **Medium**   **2 Servings**   **10 min.**   **15 min.**

Ingredients:

- 4 large eggs
- 1/2 cup cauliflower rice
- 1/2 cup spinach, chopped
- 1/2 cup shredded cheddar cheese (for the roll)
- 1/4 cup cubed cheddar cheese (for serving)
- 6-8 olives (for serving)
- 2 tablespoons heavy cream
- 1 tablespoon butter
- Salt and pepper to taste

Instructions:

1. Whisk the eggs with heavy cream, salt, and pepper. Heat butter in a skillet and pour the eggs, cooking until set in a thin layer. Transfer the egg sheet to a plate.
2. Sauté the cauliflower rice and spinach for 3-4 minutes in the same skillet.
3. Spread the sautéed vegetables over the egg sheet, sprinkle with shredded cheese, and roll the egg sheet into a log.
4. Heat a skillet over medium heat. Carefully place the rolled egg log in the skillet. Cook for 1-2 minutes on each side until the cheese inside melts and the roll is golden.
5. Slice the roll into portion-sized pieces and serve with cubed cheese and olives on the side.

Per serving:

Calories: 440 | Fats: 36g | Protein: 22g | Carbs: 6g | Net Carbs: 3g | Fiber: 3g
Fat 78% / Protein 20% / Carb 2%

KETO GREEK YOGURT WITH NUTS AND BERRIES

Ingredients:

- 1 cup unsweetened Greek yogurt (full-fat)
- 1/4 cup mixed nuts (almonds, walnuts, pecans), chopped
- 1/4 cup fresh berries (raspberries, blueberries, blackberries)
- 1 tablespoon chia seeds (optional)
- 1 tablespoon unsweetened shredded coconut (optional)
- Sweetener of choice (erythritol or stevia) to taste

Instructions:

1. In a bowl, combine the Greek yogurt and sweetener, if using.
2. Top with chopped nuts, fresh berries, chia seeds, and shredded coconut if desired.
3. Mix lightly and enjoy immediately.

Per serving:

Calories: 300 | Fats: 24g | Protein: 12g | Carbs: 9g | Net Carbs: 5g | Fiber: 4g
Fat 75% / Protein 16% / Carb 9%

Excellent **2 Servings**

Easy **5 min.** **5 min.**

CHIA SEED PUDDING WITH ALMOND MILK

Ingredients:

- 1/2 cup unsweetened almond milk
- 1/4 cup chia seeds
- 1/4 cup coconut cream (optional for added fat)
- 1 tablespoon sweetener of
- choice (erythritol or stevia)
- 1/2 teaspoon vanilla extract (optional)
- Fresh berries or nuts for topping (optional)

Instructions:

1. Mix almond milk, chia seeds, coconut cream, sweetener, and vanilla in a bowl or jar. Stir well.
2. Let sit for 5 minutes, stir again to break up clumps, then refrigerate for 2 hours or overnight.
3. Serve with fresh berries or nuts on top if desired.

Per serving:

Calories: 250 | Fats: 20g | Protein: 6g | Carbs: 10g | Net Carbs: 4g | Fiber: 6g
Fat 80% / Protein 10% / Carb 10%

Chapter 4
Appetizers and Snacks

KETO BREAD MADE FROM NUT FLOUR

Excellent

Medium

1 loaf

10 min.

40 min.

Ingredients:

- 1 cup almond flour
- 1/2 cup hazelnut flour
- 1/4 cup cashew flour
- 4 large eggs
- 1/4 cup melted butter or coconut oil

- 1 teaspoon baking powder
- 1/2 teaspoon salt
- 1 tablespoon apple cider vinegar
- 1/4 cup water
- Optional: 1 teaspoon sweetener (erythritol or stevia)

Instructions:

1. Preheat your oven to 350°F (180°C). Line a loaf pan with parchment paper or grease it with butter.

2. In a large bowl, whisk together the almond flour, hazelnut flour, cashew flour, baking powder, and salt.

3. In a separate bowl, beat the eggs and mix in the melted butter, apple cider vinegar, and water.

4. Combine the wet and dry ingredients and mix until a smooth batter forms. Pour the batter into the prepared loaf pan.

5. Bake for 35-40 minutes or until a toothpick inserted in the center comes clean. Let the bread cool for 10 minutes before slicing.

Per serving:

Calories: 200 | Fats: 18g | Protein: 6g | Carbs: 4g | Net Carbs: 2g | Fiber: 2g
Fat 82% / Protein 12% / Carb 6%

AVOCADO AND QUAIL EGG TOASTS

Ingredients:

- 1 slice keto bread made from nut flour (recipe on page 34)
- 2 quail eggs, boiled and halved
- Salt and pepper to taste
- Fresh herbs for garnish (optional)
- 1 avocado

Instructions:

1. Mash half of the avocado and spread it on the keto bread.
2. Slice the other half of the avocado and place it on top.
3. Arrange the halved quail eggs on the avocado.
4. Season with salt and pepper, and garnish with herbs if desired.

Per serving:

Calories: 300 | Fats: 26g | Protein: 7g | Carbs: 6g | Net Carbs: 3g | Fiber: 3g
Fat 78% / Protein 18% / Carb 4%

Excellent **1 Servings**

Easy **5 min.** **5 min.**

BULLETPROOF COFFEE

Ingredients:

- 1 cup brewed coffee (hot)
- 1 tablespoon MCT coconut oil
- Optional: a pinch of cinnamon or sweetener (like stevia)
- 1 tablespoon organic unsalted butter

Instructions:

1. Brew 1 cup of hot coffee.
2. Add the hot coffee, butter, and MCT coconut oil to a blender.
3. Blend for 20-30 seconds until the mixture is frothy and smooth.
4. Pour into a cup and enjoy immediately. Optionally, add cinnamon or sweetener for taste.

Per serving:

Calories: 220 | Fats: 24g | Protein: 0g | Carbs: 0g | Net Carbs: 0g | Fiber: 0g
Fat 98% / Protein 0% / Carb 0%

VEGETARIAN SMOOTHIE WITH FRESH BERRIES, AVOCADO, AND SPINACH

Excellent **Easy** **1 Servings** **10 min.** **5 min.**

Ingredients:

- 1/2 cup fresh mixed berries (strawberries, raspberries, blueberries)
- 1/2 avocado
- 1 cup spinach leaves
- 1/2 cup unsweetened almond milk

- 1 tablespoon chia seeds
- 1 tablespoon coconut oil (optional for added fat)
- Ice cubes (optional)
- Sweetener of choice (like stevia or erythritol, optional)

Instructions:

1. Place berries, avocado, spinach, and chia seeds in a blender.
2. Add almond milk, coconut oil (if using), and ice cubes (if desired).
3. Blend until smooth.
4. Taste and adjust sweetness if needed. Serve immediately.

Per serving:

Calories: 250 | Fats: 18g | Protein: 4g | Carbs: 12g | Net Carbs: 7g | Fiber: 5g
Fat 70% / Protein 10% / Carb 20%

KETO FAT BOMBS WITH COCONUT

Ingredients:

- 1/2 cup coconut oil, melted
- 1/4 cup unsweetened shredded coconut
- 1/4 cup almond butter or peanut butter (unsweetened)
- 2 tablespoons coconut flour
- 1 tablespoon powdered erythritol or stevia (optional, to taste)
- 1/2 teaspoon vanilla extract
- Pinch of salt

Instructions:

1. In a mixing bowl, mix the melted coconut oil, almond butter, coconut flour, sweetener, vanilla extract, and salt until smooth.
2. Stir in the shredded coconut.
3. Divide the mixture into 10 small silicone molds or form small balls by hand.
4. Refrigerate for 30 minutes or until firm.
5. Once set, remove from molds or enjoy the fat bombs.

Per serving:

Calories: 120 | Fats: 11g | Protein: 1g | Carbs: 2g | Net Carbs: 1g | Fiber: 1g
Fat 90% / Protein 5% / Carb 5%

Excellent   10 fat bombs

Easy   10 min.   30 min.

KETO NUTS-CHOCOLATE FAT BOMBS

Ingredients:

- 1/4 cup coconut oil, melted
- 1/4 cup almond butter or peanut butter (unsweetened)
- 2 tablespoons cocoa powder (unsweetened)
- 1/4 teaspoon vanilla extract
- 1 tablespoon powdered erythritol or stevia
- 1/4 cup mixed nuts (almonds, walnuts, hazelnuts), chopped
- Pinch of salt

Instructions:

1. In a mixing bowl, mix melted coconut oil, almond butter, cocoa powder, sweetener, vanilla extract, and salt until smooth.
2. Stir in the chopped nuts.
3. Divide the mixture into 10 small silicone molds or form small balls by hand.
4. Refrigerate for 30 minutes or until firm.
5. Once set, remove from molds or enjoy.

Per serving:

Calories: 130 | Fats: 12g | Protein: 3g | Carbs: 3g | Net Carbs: 2g | Fiber: 1g
Fat 85% / Protein 10% / Carb 5%

Excellent   **1 Servings**

Easy   **10 min.**   **30 min.**

KETOGENIC FUDGE BROWNIE

Ingredients:

- 1/2 cup almond flour
- 1/4 cup cocoa powder (unsweetened)
- 1/2 cup butter, melted
- 1/4 cup coconut oil, melted
- 3 large eggs
- 1/2 cup powdered erythritol or
- stevia (sweetener of choice)
- 1 teaspoon vanilla extract
- 1/2 teaspoon baking powder
- 1/4 teaspoon salt
- 1/2 cup sugar-free dark chocolate chips (optional)

Instructions:

1. Preheat oven to 350°F (180°C) and line an 8x8-inch baking pan with parchment paper.
2. Mix almond flour, cocoa powder, sweetener, baking powder, and salt.
3. Whisk together melted butter, coconut oil, eggs, and vanilla extract.
4. Combine wet and dry ingredients. Stir in chocolate chips if using.
5. Pour the batter into the pan and smooth the top. Bake for 20-25 minutes. Cool, then cut into 10 brownies.

Per serving:

Calories: 190 | Fats: 18g | Protein: 3g | Carbs: 4g | Net Carbs: 2g | Fiber: 2g Fat 89% / Protein 7% / Carb 4%

PUMPKIN SPICE - CACAO FAT BOMBS

Ingredients:

- 1/4 cup coconut oil, melted
- 1/4 cup almond butter or peanut butter (unsweetened)
- 2 tablespoons pumpkin puree (unsweetened)
- 1 tablespoon cocoa powder (unsweetened)
- 1 tablespoon powdered erythritol or stevia
- 1/2 teaspoon pumpkin spice mix (cinnamon, nutmeg, ginger)
- 1/2 teaspoon vanilla extract
- Pinch of salt

Instructions:

1. Mix melted coconut oil, almond butter, pumpkin puree, cocoa powder, sweetener, pumpkin spice, vanilla extract, and salt until smooth.
2. Divide the mixture into 10 small silicone molds or form small balls by hand.
3. Refrigerate for 30 minutes or until firm.
4. Once set, remove from molds or enjoy as fat bombs.

Per serving:

Calories: 100 | Fats: 9g | Protein: 2g | Carbs: 3g | Net Carbs: 2g | Fiber: 1g Fat 85% / Protein 10% / Carb 5%

KETO ALMOND FLOUR CREPES

Excellent

Medium

6 crepes

10 min.

15 min.

Ingredients:

For the Crepes:
- 1/2 cup almond flour
- 2 large eggs
- 1/4 cup unsweetened almond milk
- 2 tablespoons melted butter
- 1/2 teaspoon vanilla extract
- 1/4 cup raspberries, mashed
- Pinch of salt

For the Filling:
- 1/2 cup mascarpone cheese
- 1 tablespoon powdered erythritol or stevia (optional)
- 1/2 teaspoon vanilla extract
- Fresh raspberries for garnish

1. In a bowl, whisk together the almond flour, eggs, almond milk, melted butter, vanilla extract, mashed raspberries, and a pinch of salt until smooth.
2. Heat a non-stick skillet over medium heat and lightly grease it with butter or oil. Pour about 1/4 cup of the batter into the skillet and swirl to spread thin. Cook for 1-2 minutes on each side until golden. Repeat with the remaining batter.
3. Mix mascarpone cheese, sweetener, and vanilla extract in a separate bowl until smooth.
4. Fill each crepe with a spoonful of the mascarpone filling, fold or roll, and garnish with fresh raspberries.

Per serving:

Calories: 180 | Fats: 15g | Protein: 6g | Carbs: 4g | Net Carbs: 2g | Fiber: 2g
Fat 75% / Protein 15% / Carb 10%

KETO NUT BUTTER

Ingredients:

- 1 cup mixed nuts (almonds, walnuts, cashews, or pecans)
- 1 tablespoon coconut oil, melted
- 1/2 teaspoon vanilla extract (optional)
- 1/4 teaspoon cinnamon (optional)
- Pinch of salt

Instructions:

1. Toast the nuts in a dry skillet for 3-5 minutes until fragrant.
2. Blend the nuts in a food processor until smooth.
3. Add coconut oil, vanilla, cinnamon, and salt, and blend until creamy.
4. Store in an airtight jar and refrigerate for up to 2 weeks.

Per serving:

Calories: 190 | Fats: 18g | Protein: 4g | Carbs: 4g | Net Carbs: 2g | Fiber: 2g
Fat 90% / Protein 8% / Carb 2%

Excellent   **1 cup**

Easy   **5 min.**   **5 min.**

KETO SMOOTHIE WITH GREEN SPINACH AND ALMOND

Ingredients:

- 1 cup fresh spinach
- 1/2 cup unsweetened almond milk
- 1 tablespoon almond butter
- 1/4 avocado
- 1 tablespoon chia seeds
- 1/2 teaspoon vanilla extract (optional)
- Ice cubes (optional)
- Sweetener of choice (optional, to taste)

Instructions:

1. Combine all ingredients in a blender.
2. Blend until smooth.
3. Add ice cubes if desired and blend again.
4. Serve immediately.

Per serving:

Calories: 100 | Fats: 9g | Protein: 2g | Carbs: 3g | Net Carbs: 2g | Fiber: 1g
Fat 85% / Protein 10% / Carb 5%

Chapter 5
Soups and Salads

Greens and Arugula: Keto Nutritional Boost

Leafy greens are essential on keto, providing fiber, vitamins, and minerals with minimal carbs. Rich in antioxidants, greens support immunity and aid digestion, which is key to a low-carb diet.

Arugula is especially beneficial—low in calories and carbs, yet high in vitamins A, C, and K, which promote bone and skin health. Its peppery flavor adds freshness to salads, omelets, and keto-friendly dishes. Adding a variety of greens like arugula regularly keeps your diet nutrient-dense and satisfying.

SALAD OF TOMATOES, AVOCADO, ARUGULA, RADISH, AND SEEDS

 Excellent   **Medium**   **2 Servings**   **10 min.**   **10 min.**

Ingredients:

- 1 cup cherry tomatoes, halved
- 1 avocado, sliced into half-moons
- 2 cups arugula
- 2 radishes, thinly sliced
- 1/4 small red onion, thinly sliced
- 2 tablespoons mixed seeds (sunflower, pumpkin, sesame)
- 2 tablespoons olive oil
- 1 tablespoon lemon juice
- Salt and pepper to taste

Instructions:

1. Combine cherry tomatoes, avocado, arugula, radish, and red onion in a large bowl.
2. Drizzle with olive oil and lemon juice, and season with salt and pepper.
3. Sprinkle the mixed seeds on top.
4. Toss gently and serve immediately.

Per serving:

Calories: 310 | Fats: 28g | Protein: 4g | Carbs: 10g | Net Carbs: 5g | Fiber: 5g
Fat 80% / Protein 10% / Carb 10%

CAULIFLOWER CREAM SOUP WITH BACON

Ingredients:

- 4 cups cauliflower florets
- 2 cups chicken or vegetable broth
- 1 cup heavy cream
- 4 slices bacon, cooked and crumbled
- 2 tablespoons butter
- 1/2 cup grated Parmesan cheese
- 2 cloves garlic, minced
- Salt and pepper to taste

Instructions:

1. Melt the butter and sauté the garlic in a large pot for 1 minute.
2. Add cauliflower and broth and simmer for 10-12 minutes until tender.
3. Blend the soup until smooth. Stir in the cream and Parmesan.
4. Top each serving with crumbled bacon and season with salt and pepper. Serve hot.

Per serving:

Calories: 350 | Fats: 30g | Protein: 12g | Carbs: 6g | Net Carbs: 4g | Fiber: 2g
Fat 80% / Protein 15% / Carb 5%

Excellent   **4 Servings**

Easy   **10 min.**   **20 min.**

BROCCOLI CREAM SOUP WITH CREAM AND PARMESAN

Ingredients:

- 2 cups broccoli florets
- 2 cups chicken or vegetable broth
- 1 cup heavy cream
- 1/2 cup grated Parmesan cheese
- 2 tablespoons butter
- 2 cloves garlic, minced
- 1 tablespoon mixed seeds (sesame, pumpkin, sunflower) for garnish
- Salt and pepper to taste

Instructions:

1. Melt butter in a pot and sauté the garlic for 1 minute.
2. Add broccoli and broth, simmer for 10-12 minutes until tender.
3. Blend the soup until smooth.
4. Stir in cream and Parmesan, season with salt and pepper, and cook for 5 more minutes.
5. Top each serving with a handful of mixed seeds (sesame, pumpkin, sunflower) for garnish. Serve hot.

Per serving:

Calories: 130 | Fats: 12g | Protein: 3g | Carbs: 3g | Net Carbs: 2g | Fiber: 1g
Fat 85% / Protein 10% / Carb 5%

Soups and Broths: Keto Essentials

Soups and broths are valuable on the keto diet, offering hydration, minerals, and a warm, satisfying option with minimal carbs. High in electrolytes like sodium, potassium, and magnesium, broths help maintain nutrient balance, which is key on keto.

Bone broth is especially beneficial, containing collagen and amino acids that support joint health and digestion. A low-carb soup or broth can also keep you full and reduce cravings, making them perfect for staying on track with keto.

KETO TURKEY MEATBALL SOUP WITH ZUCCHINI NOODLES AND CARROT

 Excellent   **Medium**   **4 Servings**   **15 min.**   **25 min.**

Ingredients:

For the Meatballs:
- 1 lb ground turkey
- 1/4 cup grated Parmesan cheese
- 1 egg
- 1 teaspoon garlic powder
- 1 teaspoon dried oregano
- Salt and pepper to taste

For the Soup:
- 1 medium zucchini, sliced into
- thin, long strips (like noodles)
- 1 large carrot, sliced into rounds
- 4 cups chicken or vegetable broth
- 2 tablespoons olive oil
- 1 small onion, diced
- 2 cloves garlic, minced
- Salt and pepper to taste

Instructions:

1. Mix the ground turkey, Parmesan, egg, garlic powder, oregano, salt, and pepper. Form small meatballs and lightly brown them in 1 tablespoon olive oil for 3-4 minutes. Remove them from the pot and set aside.
2. In the same pot, bring the broth to a boil. Add the carrot slices and cook for 10 minutes.
3. Gently add the partially cooked meatballs to the broth and simmer for 10 minutes.
4. Stir in the zucchini strips and cook for the final 3-4 minutes, until tender but not mushy. Season with salt and pepper, then serve.

Per serving:

Calories: 450 | Fats: 35g | Protein: 22g | Carbs: 6g | Net Carbs: 4g | Fiber: 2g
Fat 74% / Protein 22% / Carb 4%

CREAM OF MUSHROOM SOUP

Ingredients:

- 2 cups mushrooms, sliced
- 1 small onion, diced
- 2 cloves garlic, minced
- 2 cups chicken or vegetable broth
- 1 cup heavy cream
- 2 tablespoons butter
- 1/4 cup grated Parmesan cheese
- Salt and pepper to taste
- 8 mushroom slices, pan-fried (for garnish)

Instructions:

1. Melt butter in a pot and sauté the mushrooms, onion, and garlic for 5-7 minutes until softened.
2. Add the broth, bring to a simmer, and cook for 10 minutes.
3. Stir in the heavy cream and Parmesan, season with salt and pepper, and simmer for 5 more minutes.
4. Blend the soup to your desired consistency. Garnish each bowl with 2 slices of pan-fried mushrooms. Serve hot.

Per serving:

Calories: 350 | Fats: 30g | Protein: 12g | Carbs: 6g | Net Carbs: 4g | Fiber: 2g
Fat 80% / Protein 15% / Carb 5%

Excellent   **4 Servings**

Easy   **10 min.**   **20 min.**

SALAD OF FRESH VEGETABLES, GRILLED SHRIMP, AND QUAIL EGGS

Ingredients:

- 2 cups mushrooms, sliced
- 1 small onion, diced
- 2 cloves garlic, minced
- 2 cups chicken or vegetable broth
- 1 cup heavy cream
- 2 tablespoons butter
- 1/4 cup grated Parmesan cheese
- Salt and pepper to taste
- 8 mushroom slices, pan-fried (for garnish)

Instructions:

1. Melt butter in a pot and sauté the mushrooms, onion, and garlic for 5-7 minutes until softened.
2. Add the broth, bring to a simmer, and cook for 10 minutes.
3. Stir in the heavy cream and Parmesan, season with salt and pepper, and simmer for 5 more minutes.
4. Blend the soup to your desired consistency. Garnish each bowl with 2 slices of pan-fried mushrooms. Serve hot.

Per serving:

Calories: 130 | Fats: 12g | Protein: 3g | Carbs: 3g | Net Carbs: 2g | Fiber: 1g
Fat 85% / Protein 10% / Carb 5%

GREEK SALAD

Ingredients:

- 1 cup cherry tomatoes, halved
- 1 cucumber, diced
- 1/4 small red onion, thinly sliced
- 1/2 cup feta cheese, crumbled
- 1/4 cup Kalamata olives

- 2 tablespoons olive oil
- 1 tablespoon red wine vinegar
- 1 teaspoon dried oregano
- Salt and pepper to taste

Instructions:

1. Combine cherry tomatoes, cucumber, red onion, feta cheese, and Kalamata olives in a large bowl.
2. Drizzle with olive oil, and red wine vinegar, and sprinkle with dried oregano.
3. Season with salt and pepper to taste.
4. Toss gently and serve immediately.

Per serving:

Calories: 300 | Fats: 25g | Protein: 8g | Carbs: 7g | Net Carbs: 4g | Fiber: 3g
Fat 80% / Protein 15% / Carb 5%

Excellent   2 Servings

Easy   10 min.   15 min.

CHICKEN BREAST SALAD WITH ZUCCHINI, CHERRY TOMATOES, AND ARUGULA

Ingredients:

- 1 cup fresh arugula
- 1 cup cherry tomatoes, halved
- 1 tablespoon mixed seeds (optional, for garnish)
- 1 medium chicken breast (about 6 oz), cooked and sliced

- 2 tablespoons olive oil
- 1 tablespoon lemon juice
- 1/4 cup fresh basil leaves
- Salt and pepper to taste
- 1 small zucchini, sliced into thin rounds

Instructions:

1. Sauté zucchini in 1 tablespoon olive oil for 3-4 minutes.
2. Combine chicken, zucchini, cherry tomatoes, arugula, and basil in a bowl.
3. Drizzle with the remaining olive oil, lemon juice, salt, and pepper.
4. Toss gently, garnish with seeds, and serve.

Per serving:

Calories: 330 | Fats: 26g | Protein: 20g | Carbs: 6g | Net Carbs: 4g | Fiber: 2g
Fat 75% / Protein 18% / Carb 7%

Tuna: A Keto-Friendly Protein Boost

Tuna is an excellent source of lean protein and healthy fats, making it perfect for the keto diet. Low in carbs and high in essential nutrients like omega-3 fatty acids, selenium, and vitamin D, tuna supports heart health, brain function, and immunity.

Canned tuna is especially convenient—adding to salads, wraps, or keto-friendly casseroles is easy for a quick, nutritious meal. Including tuna in your diet a few times a week helps you meet protein needs and adds variety to your keto meals without excess carbs.

TUNA SALAD WITH CHERRY TOMATOES AND GREENS

Excellent **Easy** **2 Servings** **15 min.** **5 min.**

Ingredients:

- 1 can (5 oz) tuna in olive oil, drained
- 1 cup cherry tomatoes, halved
- 1/4 red onion, thinly sliced
- 2 hard-boiled eggs, chopped
- 1 teaspoon paprika

- 2 cups lettuce, chopped
- 1 cup radicchio, chopped
- 1 cup arugula
- 2 tablespoons olive oil
- 1 tablespoon lemon juice
- Salt and pepper to taste

Instructions:

1. Combine the tuna, cherry tomatoes, red onion, hard-boiled eggs, sweet corn, and paprika in a large bowl.
2. Whisk together olive oil, lemon juice, salt, and pepper in a separate bowl.
3. Pour the dressing over the tuna mixture and toss gently to combine.
4. Serve the tuna salad over a bed of mixed greens, including lettuce, radicchio, and arugula.

Per serving:

Calories: 320 | Fats: 25g | Protein: 24g | Carbs: 6g | Net Carbs: 4g | Fiber: 2g
Fat 75% / Protein 30% / Carb 5%

AVOCADO EGGS SALAD

Ingredients:

- 4 hard-boiled eggs, chopped
- 1 large avocado, diced
- 1 tablespoon mayonnaise
- 1 tablespoon lemon juice
- 1 teaspoon Dijon mustard
- 1 tablespoon fresh parsley, chopped (optional)
- Salt and pepper to tasteg

Instructions:

1. In a bowl, combine chopped eggs and diced avocado.
2. Add mayonnaise, lemon juice, Dijon mustard, and mix gently.
3. Season with salt and pepper, and garnish with fresh parsley if desired.
4. Serve immediately or chill in the fridge for later.

Per serving:

Calories: 300 | Fats: 25g | Protein: 8g | Carbs: 7g | Net Carbs: 4g | Fiber: 3g
Fat 80% / Protein 15% / Carb 5%

Excellent 2 Servings

Easy 10 min. 10 min.

GROUND BEEF CABBAGE SOUP

Ingredients:

- 1 lb ground beef
- 1/2 head of cabbage, chopped
- 1 red bell pepper, diced
- 1 small onion, diced
- 2 cloves garlic, minced
- 1 cup diced tomatoes (fresh or canned)
- 4 cups beef broth
- 2 tablespoons olive oil
- 1 teaspoon paprika
- Salt and pepper to taste
- 1/4 cup fresh coriander (cilantro), chopped

Instructions:

1. Heat olive oil in a large pot and sauté the onion, garlic, and red bell pepper for 3-4 minutes.
2. Add the ground beef and cook until browned, about 5-6 minutes.
3. Stir in the chopped cabbage, diced tomatoes, paprika, salt, and pepper. Pour in the beef broth and bring to a simmer.
4. Cook for 20-25 minutes until the cabbage is tender. Garnish with fresh coriander and serve.

Per serving:

Calories: 350 | Fats: 23g | Protein: 20g | Carbs: 8g | Net Carbs: 6g | Fiber: 2g
Fat 70% / Protein 25% / Carb 5%

Chapter 6
Fish and Seafood

Salmon: A Keto Superfood

Salmon is a powerhouse for the keto diet, offering rich, healthy fats and high-quality protein with minimal carbs. Packed with omega-3 fatty acids, vitamin D, and B vitamins, salmon supports heart health, brain function, and immune strength, which are essential for overall wellness.

Its healthy fats help maintain energy levels on keto, making it a satisfying meal choice. Whether grilled, baked, or smoked, salmon adds flavor and nutrition to various keto meals, providing nutrients that keep you full and energized.

BAKED SALMON WITH ASPARAGUS

 Excellent **Easy** **2 Servings** **10 min.** **15 min.**

Ingredients:

- 2 salmon fillets (about 6 oz each)
- 1/2 lb asparagus, trimmed
- 2 tablespoons olive oil
- 1 tablespoon lemon juice
- 1 teaspoon garlic powder

- 1 teaspoon dried thyme
- Salt and pepper to taste
- 1 tablespoon butter (for finishing)
- 6 fresh mushrooms
- Fresh blueberries for garnish

Instructions:

1. Preheat the oven to 400°F (200°C). Line a baking sheet with parchmen paper.
2. Arrange the salmon fillets and asparagus on the baking sheet. Drizzle wit olive oil and lemon juice, and season with garlic powder, thyme, salt, anc pepper.
3. Bake in the preheated oven for 12-15 minutes until the salmon is cooked and flakes easily with a fork and the asparagus is tender.
4. While the salmon and asparagus are baking, heat 1 tablespoon of olive o in a skillet over medium heat and sauté the mushrooms for 3-4 minute: until golden brown.
5. Remove from the oven and top the salmon with a pat of butter. Let it mel before serving.
6. Garnish the salmon and asparagus with fresh blueberries and sesame seeds and serve immediately.

Per serving:

Calories: 450 | Fats: 35g | Protein: 30g | Carbs: 5g | Net Carbs: 3g | Fiber: 2g
Fat 70% / Protein 27% / Carb 3%

SHRIMP WITH GARLIC AND DILL

Shrimp: A Keto-Friendly Protein Source

Shrimp is an ideal addition to the keto diet, offering high-quality protein with almost no carbs. Low in calories yet rich in nutrients like selenium, B12, and iodine, shrimp supports thyroid health, energy, and immunity—key for overall wellness on keto.

The lean protein in shrimp satisfies hunger without excess fat, making it perfect for salads, stir-fries, or appetizers. With their mild flavor, shrimp pairs well with many keto dishes, adding nutrition and variety.

Excellent　**Easy**　**2 Servings**　**10 min.**　**10 min.**

Ingredients:

- 1/2 lb shrimp, peeled and deveined
- 2 tablespoons butter
- 2 cloves garlic, minced
- 1 tablespoon fresh dill, chopped
- 1 tablespoon lemon juice
- Salt and pepper to taste
- Fresh dill for garnish (optional)

Instructions:

1. Heat butter in a large skillet over medium heat. Add the minced garlic and sauté for about 30 seconds until fragrant.
2. Add the shrimp to the skillet and cook for 2-3 minutes per side, until pink and opaque.
3. Stir in the lemon juice, fresh dill, salt, and pepper. Cook for an additional minute to combine the flavors.
4. Remove from heat, garnish with extra fresh dill if desired, and serve immediately.

Per serving:

Calories: 250 | Fats: 20g | Protein: 18g | Carbs: 1g | Net Carbs: 1g | Fiber: 0g
Fat 75% / Protein 24% / Carb 1%

GRILLED TUNA STEAK WITH PEPPER AND AVOCADO CUCUMBER SALSA

Excellent   **Medium**   **2 Servings**   **10 min.**   **10 min.**

Ingredients:

For the Tuna Steaks:
- 2 tuna steaks (6 oz each)
- 1 tablespoon olive oil
- 1 teaspoon garlic powder
- 1 teaspoon paprika
- Salt and pepper to taste

For the Avocado Cucumber Salsa:
- 1 ripe avocado, diced
- 1/2 cup cucumber, diced
- 1/4 cup red bell pepper, diced
- 1 tablespoon lime juice
- 1 tablespoon olive oil
- Salt and pepper to taste

Instructions:

1. Preheat the oven to 400°F (200°C) and turn on the grill (broiler) function. Rub the tuna steaks with olive oil, garlic powder, paprika, salt, and pepper.
2. Place the tuna steaks on a grill rack or baking tray lined with foil. Grill for 4-5 minutes per side, depending on your preferred doneness. Remove and let rest for a few minutes.
3. Mix the diced avocado, cucumber, red bell pepper, lime juice, and olive oil in a bowl—season with salt and pepper.
4. Serve the grilled tuna steaks with the avocado cucumber salsa on the side.

Per serving:

Calories: 420 | Fats: 32g | Protein: 30g | Carbs: 6g | Net Carbs: 4g | Fiber: 2g
Fat 70% / Protein 28% / Carb 2%

BAKED ATLANTIC SALMON

Ingredients:

- 2 Atlantic salmon fillets (6 oz each)
- 2 tablespoons olive oil
- 1 tablespoon lemon juice
- Salt and pepper to taste
- 1 teaspoon garlic powder
- 1 teaspoon paprika

Instructions:

1. Preheat the oven to 400°F (200°C).
2. Place the salmon fillets on a baking sheet lined with parchment paper. Drizzle with olive oil and lemon juice, and season with garlic powder, paprika, salt, and pepper.
3. Bake for 12-15 minutes, until the salmon flakes easily with a fork.
4. Serve coarsely chopped baked salmon with avocado and tomato salsa (recipe on page 59).

Per serving:

Calories: 400 | Fats: 34g | Protein: 28g | Carbs: 2g | Net Carbs: 1g | Fiber: 1g
Fat 75% / Protein 23% / Carb 2%

Excellent 2 Servings

Medium 10 min. 15 min.

BAKED SEABASS

Ingredients:

- 2 seabass fillets (6 oz each)
- 2 tablespoons olive oil
- 1 tablespoon lemon juice
- 1 teaspoon dried oregano
- Salt and pepper to taste

Instructions:

1. Preheat the oven to 400°F (200°C).
2. Place the seabass fillets on a lined baking sheet. Drizzle with olive oil and lemon juice and sprinkle with oregano, salt, and pepper.
3. Bake for 12-15 minutes until the fish is cooked and flakes easily with a fork.
4. Remove from the oven and rest for a couple of minutes before serving.

Per serving:

Calories: 320 | Fats: 28g | Protein: 20g | Carbs: 1g | Net Carbs: 1g | Fiber: 0g
Fat 75% / Protein 24% / Carb 1%

CASSEROLE WITH SALMON AND BROCCOLI

Excellent   **Medium**   **2 Servings**   **15 min.**   **25 min.**

Ingredients:

- 8 oz salmon fillets, skinless and boneless
- 1 cup broccoli florets
- 1/2 cup heavy cream
- 1/2 cup shredded cheddar cheese

- 2 large eggs
- 1 tablespoon olive oil
- 1/4 teaspoon garlic powder
- 1/4 teaspoon paprika
- Salt and pepper to taste

Instructions:

1. Preheat the oven to 375°F (190°C) and grease a small baking dish with olive oil.

2. Steam the broccoli florets for 3-4 minutes until slightly tender. Set aside.

3. In a bowl, whisk together the eggs, heavy cream, garlic powder, paprika, salt, and pepper.

4. Cut the salmon into bite-sized pieces and layer them evenly in the baking dish. Add the steamed broccoli florets on top.

5. Pour the egg and cream mixture over the salmon and broccoli, ensuring everything is well coated. Sprinkle the shredded cheddar cheese on top.

6. Bake for 20-25 minutes or until the casserole is set and the cheese is golden and bubbly.

7. Let the casserole cool for a few minutes before serving.

Per serving:

Calories: 500 | Fats: 40g | Protein: 28g | Carbs: 6g | Net Carbs: 4g | Fiber: 2g
Fat 72% / Protein 25% / Carb 3%

WHITE FISH ALASKAN POLLOCK WITH SPINACH

Ingredients:

- 2 Alaskan pollock fillets (6 oz each)
- 2 tablespoons olive oil
- 1 tablespoon lemon juice
- 1 teaspoon garlic powder
- Salt and pepper to taste

Instructions:

1. Preheat the oven to 400°F (200°C). Drizzle the pollock fillets with olive oil and lemon juice. Season with garlic powder, salt, and pepper. Place on a lined baking sheet.
2. Bake for 12-15 minutes until the fish is cooked through and flakes easily with a fork.
3. Remove from the oven and let the fish rest for a few minutes.
4. Serve the baked pollock with sautéed spinach (recipe on page 78).

Per serving:

Calories: 280 | Fats: 22g | Protein: 25g | Carbs: 2g | Net Carbs: 1g | Fiber: 1g
Fat 70% / Protein 28% / Carb 2%

Excellent   **2 Servings**

Medium   **10 min.**   **15 min.**

FRIED TILAPIA FISH FILLET WITH AVOCADO AND VEGETABLES

Ingredients:

- 2 tilapia fillets (6 oz each)
- 2 tablespoons coconut oil
- 1 teaspoon garlic powder
- 1/2 teaspoon paprika
- Salt and pepper to taste
- 1 ripe avocado, diced
- 1/2 cup cucumber, diced
- 1/2 cup tomatoes, diced
- 1 tablespoon lemon juice

Instructions:

1. Pat the fillets dry and season with garlic powder, paprika, salt, and pepper.
2. Heat the coconut oil in a skillet over medium heat. Fry the fillets for 3-4 minutes per side until golden and cooked through.
3. In a bowl, mix diced avocado, cucumber, and tomatoes. Drizzle with lemon juice and season with salt and pepper.
4. Serve the fried tilapia with the avocado and vegetable mix.

Per serving:

Calories: 400 | Fats: 32g | Protein: 22g | Carbs: 6g | Net Carbs: 4g | Fiber: 2g
Fat 75% / Protein 22% / Carb 3%

COD FILLET BAKED WITH GARLIC BUTTER SAUCE

Excellent

Medium

2 Servings

10 min.

15 min.

Ingredients:

- 2 cod fillets (6 oz each)
- 2 tablespoons butter, melted
- 2 cloves garlic, minced
- 1 tablespoon lemon juice

- 1 teaspoon fresh parsley, chopped
- 1/4 teaspoon paprika
- Salt and pepper to taste

Instructions:

1. Preheat the oven to 400°F (200°C). Line a baking dish with parchment paper.

2. Mix the melted butter, minced garlic, lemon juice, parsley, paprika, salt, and pepper in a small bowl.

3. Place the cod fillets in the baking dish. Pour the garlic butter sauce over the fillets, ensuring they are evenly coated.

4. Bake for 12-15 minutes until the cod is cooked and flakes easily with a fork.

5. Serve with asparagus (recipe on page 78).

Per serving:

Calories: 350 | Fats: 30g | Protein: 22g | Carbs: 2g | Net Carbs: 1g | Fiber: 1g
Fat 75% / Protein 23% / Carb 2%

Chapter 7
Poultry

CHICKEN MEATBALLS WITH TOMATOES

Excellent	**Medium**	**2 Servings**	**15 min.**	**15 min.**

Ingredients:

- 1 lb (450 g) ground chicken
- 1/4 cup almond flour
- 1 large egg
- 2 cloves garlic, minced
- 1 teaspoon dried oregano
- 1 teaspoon onion powder
- Salt and pepper to taste

- Salt and pepper to taste
- 1 cup tomatoes, finely chopped
- 2 tablespoons fresh herbs (such as parsley or basil), finely chopped
- 2 tablespoons olive oil

Instructions:

1. Combine ground chicken, almond flour, egg, garlic, oregano, onion powder, salt, pepper, chopped tomatoes, and herbs in a bowl. Mix until well combined.
2. Form the mixture into small meatballs or patties.
3. Heat olive oil in a skillet over medium heat. Add the meatballs and cook for 5-7 minutes on each side until golden brown and cooked through.
4. Serve hot, garnished with additional fresh herbs if desired.

Per serving:

Calories: 400 | Fats: 30g | Protein: 35g | Carbs: 6g | Net Carbs: 3g | Fiber: 3g
Fat 75% / Protein 25% / Carb 5%

CHICKEN BREASTS WITH PESTO SAUCE

Poultry: A Lean Protein Essential for Keto

Poultry, especially chicken breast, is a fantastic option on the keto diet, providing lean protein with minimal carbs and fats. Rich in B vitamins, selenium, and phosphorus, poultry supports metabolism, energy, and muscle health, all important for staying strong on keto.

Chicken breast is low in calories but filling, making it an ideal choice for meals that meet protein needs without adding excess fat. Versatile and mild in flavor, poultry pairs well with keto sides, keeping your meals nutritious and satisfying.

Excellent   **2 Servings**   **Easy**   **10 min.**   **20 min.**

Ingredients:

- 1 lb (450 g) chicken breasts (about 2 pieces)
- 1/4 cup pesto sauce (store-bought or homemade)
- 2 tablespoons olive oil
- Salt and pepper to taste
- Fresh basil leaves for garnish (optional)

Instructions:

1. Preheat the oven to 375°F (190°C).
2. Rub the chicken breasts with olive oil, salt, pepper, and half of the pesto sauce. Place them in a baking dish.
3. Bake the chicken for 20 minutes or until cooked through.
4. Remove from the oven and let the chicken rest for a few minutes.
5. Before serving, generously coat the chicken with the remaining pesto sauce and garnish with fresh basil if desired.

Per serving:

Calories: 400 | Fats: 30g | Protein: 36g | Carbs: 4g| Net Carbs: 2g | Fiber: 2g
Fat 75% / Protein 25% / Carb 5%

60

TURKEY MEATLOAF ROLL WITH SAUTÉED MUSHROOMS AND CHEESE

Ingredients:

- 1 lb (450 g) ground turkey
- 4 large mushrooms, chopped
- 1/4 cup onion, chopped
- 1/2 cup shredded cheese
- 1/4 cup almond flour
- 1 tablespoon olive oil
- 1 large egg
- 1 teaspoon garlic powder
- 1 teaspoon onion powder
- Salt and pepper to taste
- 1/4 cup grated Parmesan cheese

Instructions:

1. Preheat the oven to 375°F (190°C).
2. Sauté the mushrooms and onion in olive oil until soft, about 5 minutes—season with salt and pepper.
3. In a bowl, mix ground turkey, almond flour, egg, garlic powder, onion powder, salt, and pepper.
4. Spread the turkey mixture into a rectangle on a parchment-lined baking sheet. Top with sautéed mushrooms and cheese.
5. Roll the turkey mixture into a log and bake for 25-30 minutes until cooked through. Let rest, slice.

Per serving:

Calories: 300 | Fats: 25g | Protein: 8g | Carbs: 7g | Net Carbs: 4g | Fiber: 3g
Fat 80% / Protein 15% / Carb 5%

Excellent   2 Servings

Medium   15 min.   30 min.

GRILLED TURKEY BREAST WITH AVOCADO, CUCUMBER, AND HERB MAYO

Ingredients:

- 1 lb (450 g) turkey breast
- 2 tablespoons olive oil
- 1 teaspoon garlic powder
- Salt and pepper to taste
- 1 ripe avocado, sliced
- 1 cucumber, sliced
- 1/4 cup mayonnaise (store-bought)
- 2 tablespoons fresh herbs (parsley, dill, or cilantro), chopped
- Fresh herbs for garnish

Instructions:

1. Preheat the grill to medium-high heat.
2. Rub the turkey breast with olive oil, garlic powder, salt, and pepper.
3. Grill the turkey on each side for 10-12 minutes or until cooked through.
4. Let the turkey rest for a few minutes, then slice.
5. In a small bowl, mix the mayonnaise with chopped herbs.
6. Serve the sliced turkey on a plate with avocado, cucumber, and a dollop of herb mayo. Garnish with additional herbs if desired.

Per serving:

Calories: 450 | Fats: 35g | Protein: 32g | Carbs: 6g | Net Carbs: 3g | Fiber: 3g
Fat 75% / Protein 25% / Carb 5%

STIR FRY WITH CHICKEN AND ASPARAGUS

Asparagus: A Keto-Friendly Low-Carb Vegetable

Asparagus is a great keto choice, providing fiber, antioxidants, and essential vitamins with very few carbs. Rich in vitamins A, C, and K, along with folate, asparagus supports immunity, bone health, and cellular function—all important for keto. Its high fiber aids digestion and helps keep you full, while its low-calorie count allows for generous portions. With a mild taste and versatile texture, asparagus works well in keto dishes, from stir-fries to roasted sides.

Excellent **2 Servings** **Easy** **10 min.** **20 min.**

Ingredients:

- 1 bunch asparagus, trimmed and cut into 2-inch pieces
- 1 tablespoon coconut aminos
- 1 tablespoon sesame seeds
- 1 lb (450 g) chicken breast, sliced
- 1 teaspoon ginger, minced
- Salt and pepper to taste
- 2 tablespoons olive oil
- 2 cloves garlic, minced
- 1-2 green onions, finely chopped for garnish

Instructions:

1. Heat olive oil in a large skillet or wok over medium-high heat.
2. Add sliced chicken and stir-fry for 5-6 minutes until cooked.
3. Add garlic, ginger, and asparagus to the skillet. Stir-fry for an additional 4-5 minutes until the asparagus is tender-crisp.
4. Drizzle with coconut aminos and season with salt and pepper. Stir well to combine.
5. Serve hot, garnished with sesame seeds and chopped green onions.

Per serving:

Calories: 400 | Fats: 30g | Protein: 36g | Carbs: 4g| Net Carbs: 2g| Fiber 2g
Fat 75% / Protein 25% / Carb 5%

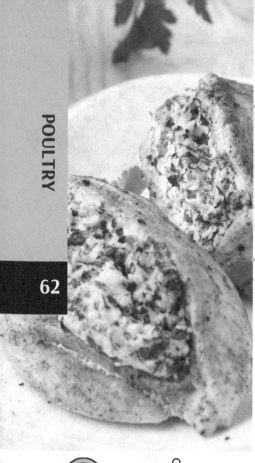

CHICKEN FILLET STUFFED WITH COTTAGE CHEESE, RICOTTA, AND HERBS

Ingredients:

- 2 chicken fillets
- 1/2 cup cottage cheese
- 1/2 cup ricotta cheese
- 1/4 cup fresh parsley, chopped
- 1 tablespoon fresh basil, chopped
- 1 teaspoon garlic powder
- 1 teaspoon onion powder
- Salt and pepper to taste
- 2 tablespoons olive oil
- 1/2 cup grated Parmesan cheese (for topping, optional)

Instructions:

1. Preheat the oven to 375°F (190°C).
2. In a bowl, mix cottage cheese, ricotta, parsley, basil, garlic powder, onion powder, salt, and pepper.
3. Cut pockets in the chicken fillets and stuff with the cheese mixture.
4. Heat olive oil in a skillet and sear the chicken for 3-4 minutes on each side until golden brown.
5. Transfer to a baking dish, top with Parmesan if desired, and bake for 15-20 minutes until cooked through.

Per serving:

Calories: 400 | Fats: 28g | Protein: 38g | Carbs: 6g | Net Carbs: 4g | Fiber: 2g
Fat 70% / Protein 30% / Carb 5%

Excellent   **2 Servings**

Medium **15 min.** **25 min.**

CHICKEN BREAST ROLL WITH BACON, CHEESE, AND DILL

Ingredients:

- 1 lb (450 g) chicken breasts
- 4 slices of bacon, cooked
- 3 tablespoons cream cheese, softened
- 2 tablespoons shredded cheddar cheese
- 2 tablespoons fresh dill, chopped
- 1 tablespoon olive oil
- Salt and pepper to taste
- Sliced avocado and tomatoes for serving

Instructions:

1. Preheat your oven to 375°F (190°C).
2. Flatten the chicken breasts with a meat mallet and season with salt and pepper.
3. Spread with cream cheese and sprinkle chicken with cheddar cheese and dill. Top with a layer of cooked bacon.
4. Roll the chicken tightly and secure it with toothpicks. Brush with olive oil.
5. Bake for 25-30 minutes until tender. Serve sliced, garnished with avocado and tomato slices.

Per serving:

Calories: 450 | Fats: 35g | Protein: 30g | Carbs: 4g | Net Carbs: 2g | Fiber: 2g
Fat 75% / Protein 25% / Carb 5%

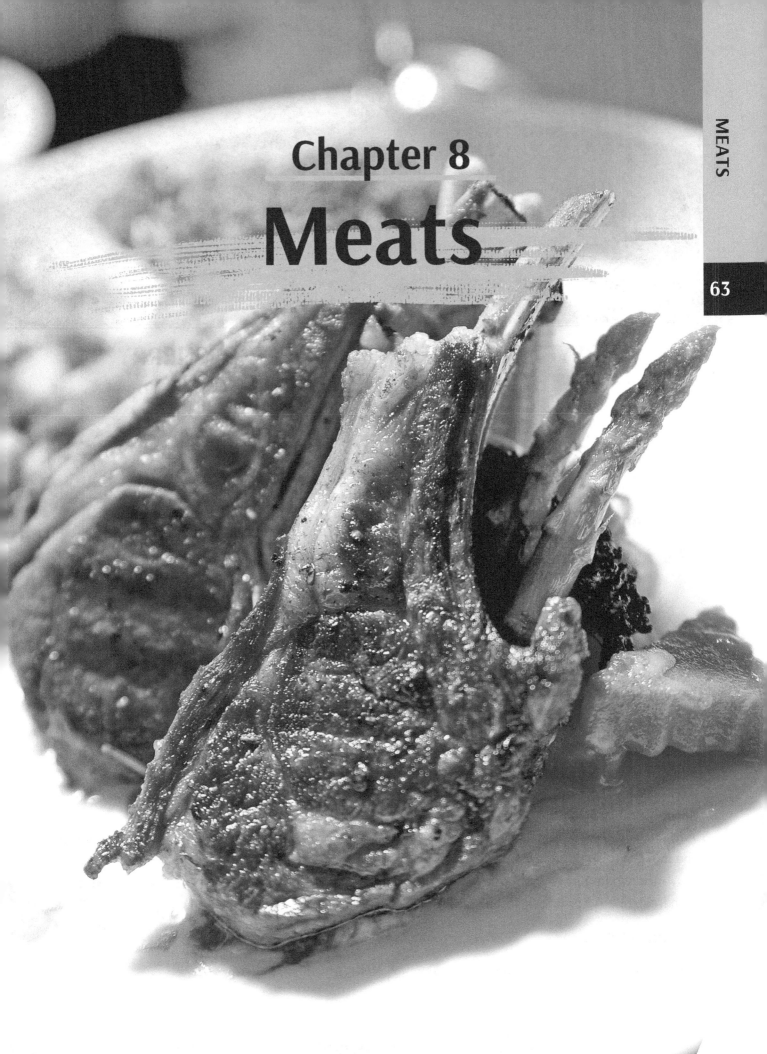

Chapter 8
Meats

RIBEYE STEAK WITH MUSHROOMS, CHERRY TOMATOES, AND ASPARAGUS

 Excellent    **Medium**   **2 Servings**   **15 min.**   **20 min.**

Ingredients:

- 2 ribeye steaks (about 8 oz each)
- 1/2 lb asparagus, trimmed
- 1/2 cup mushrooms, sliced
- 1/2 cup cherry tomatoes, halved (served fresh)
- 3 tablespoons olive oil or butter (for cooking)
- 2 cloves garlic, minced
- Salt and pepper to taste
- 1 tablespoon fresh parsley for garnish (optional)

Instructions:

1. Season the ribeye steaks generously with salt and pepper. Heat 2 tablespoons of olive oil (or butter) in a large skillet over medium-high heat. Cook the steaks on each side for 7-8 minutes for medium-rare, or longer if desired. Remove from the skillet and set aside to rest.
2. Add 1 tablespoon of olive oil (or butter) in the same skillet. Add the minced garlic and sauté for 30 seconds until fragrant.
3. Add the mushrooms and asparagus to the skillet. Sauté for 5-7 minutes until the asparagus is tender and the mushrooms are golden.
4. Serve the whole ribeye steak with the sautéed mushrooms and asparagus. If desired, garnish the plate with fresh cherry tomatoes and parsley. Serve immediately.

Per serving:

Calories: 500 | Fats: 38g | Protein: 35g | Carbs: 8g | Net Carbs: 4g | Fiber: 4g
% / Protein 27% / Carb 3%

ROASTED LAMB CHOPS

Lamb: A Nutritious Keto Protein

Lamb, especially young lamb, is a great addition to the keto diet, offering quality protein and healthy fats. Rich in iron, zinc, and B vitamins, it supports muscle function, immunity, and energy—all essential for keto.

The fats in lamb help maintain fullness and steady energy, making it a satisfying choice with its tender texture and rich flavor; young lamb pairs well with herbs and low-carb veggies, adding variety and nutrition to keto meals.

 Excellent   **Medium**   **2 Servings**   **10 min.**   **25 min.**

Ingredients:

- 4 lamb chops (about 6 oz each)
- 2 tablespoons olive oil
- 2 cloves garlic, minced
- 1 teaspoon dried rosemary
- 1 teaspoon dried thyme
- Salt and pepper to taste
- 1 tablespoon butter (for finishing)

Instructions:

1. Mix the olive oil, minced garlic, rosemary, thyme, salt, and pepper in a small bowl. Rub this mixture all over the lamb chops and let them marinate for at least 20 minutes.
2. Preheat the oven to 400°F (200°C).
3. Heat a large oven-safe skillet over medium-high heat. Sear the lamb chops on each side for 3-4 minutes until they develop a golden-brown crust.
4. Transfer the skillet to the preheated oven and roast the lamb chops for 10-12 minutes, depending on your preferred level of doneness (10 minutes for medium-rare, 12 minutes for medium).
5. Remove the skillet from the oven and add a tablespoon of butter to the hot lamb chops, allowing it to melt over them. Let the chops rest for 5 minutes before serving.

Per serving:

Calories: 450 | Fats: 34g | Protein: 30g | Carbs: 2g | Net Carbs: 2g | Fiber: 0g
Fat 75% / Protein 24% / Carb 1%

BRAISED PORK SPARE RIBS

Excellent   **Medium**   **4 Servings**   **15 min.**   **2 hours**

Ingredients:

- 1 teaspoon dried thyme
- 1 small onion, finely chopped
- 2 tablespoons olive oil or butter
- 2 lbs pork spare ribs, cut into sections
- 1/2 cup water

- 1/2 cup beef broth
- 4 cloves garlic, minced
- Salt and pepper to taste
- 1 teaspoon dried rosemary
- 2 tablespoons apple cider vinegar

Instructions:

1. Preheat your oven to 325°F (160°C).
2. Heat olive oil (or butter) in a large oven-safe skillet or Dutch oven over medium heat. Season the pork spare ribs generously with salt and pepper. Sear the ribs for 3-4 minutes per side until browned. Remove the ribs and set aside.
3. In the same skillet, add the chopped onion and garlic and sauté for 3-4 minutes until softened. Stir in the thyme, rosemary, beef broth, water, and apple cider vinegar.
4. Return the seared ribs to the skillet, ensuring they are partly submerged in the liquid. Cover the skillet tightly with a lid or foil, then transfer it to the preheated oven.
5. Braise the ribs in the oven for 1.5 to 2 hours or until the meat is tender and falling off the bone.
6. Remove from the oven and allow the ribs to rest for a few minutes before serving.

Per serving:

Calories: 500 | Fats: 40g | Protein: 28g | Carbs: 3g | Net Carbs: 2g | Fiber: 1g
5% / Protein 23% / Carb 2%

PORK TENDERLOIN WITH MUSTARD SAUCE

 Excellent **Medium** **4 Servings** **10 min.** **30 min.**

Ingredients:

- 1 lb pork tenderloin
- 2 tablespoons olive oil or butter
- Salt and pepper to taste
- 1 tablespoon fresh thyme (or 1 teaspoon dried thyme)
- For the Mustard Sauce:
- 1/2 cup heavy cream

- 2 tablespoons Dijon mustard
- 1 tablespoon whole-grain mustard
- 1 teaspoon apple cider vinegar
- 1 tablespoon butter
- Salt and pepper to taste

Instructions:

1. Preheat the oven to 400°F (200°C). Season the pork tenderloin with salt, pepper, and thyme.
2. In an oven-safe skillet, heat olive oil or butter over medium heat. Sear the pork tenderloin on each side for 3-4 minutes until browned.
3. Transfer the skillet to the oven and roast the tenderloin for 15-20 minutes or until the internal temperature reaches 145°F (63°C). Let the meat rest for 5 minutes before slicing.
4. While the pork is roasting, prepare the mustard sauce. In a small saucepan, melt butter over medium heat. Add the heavy cream, Dijon, whole-grain, and apple cider vinegar. Stir well and let simmer for 2-3 minutes until the sauce thickens—season with salt and pepper to taste.
5. Slice the pork tenderloin and drizzle with the mustard sauce. Serve immediately.

Per serving:

Calories: 350 | Fats: 28g | Protein: 22g | Carbs: 2g | Net Carbs: 2g | Fiber: 0g
Fat 70% / Protein 27% / Carb 3%

BEEF TENDERLOIN WITH CREAMY SPINACH

Excellent   **Medium**   **4 Servings**   **10 min.**   **25 min.**

Ingredients:

For the Beef Tenderloin:
- 1 lb beef tenderloin (whole piece)
- 2 tablespoons olive oil
- Salt and pepper to taste
- 1 teaspoon garlic powder
- 1 teaspoon paprika

For the Creamy Spinach:
- 2 tablespoons butter
- 1 clove garlic, minced
- 6 cups fresh spinach (about 12 oz)
- 1/2 cup heavy cream
- 1/4 cup grated Parmesan cheese
- Salt and pepper to taste

Instructions:

1. Prepare the Tenderloin: Rub the beef tenderloin with olive oil, garlic powder, paprika, salt, and pepper. Let it marinate for 10 minutes.
2. Preheat the oven to 400°F (200°C). Heat a skillet over medium-high heat and sear the tenderloin on all sides for 2-3 minutes until browned. Transfer the skillet to the oven and roast for 15-20 minutes, or until the internal temperature reaches 130°F (54°C) for medium-rare. Let the meat rest for 5 minutes before slicing.
3. Prepare the Creamy Spinach: Melt the butter in a large skillet over medium heat. Add the minced garlic and sauté for 30 seconds until fragrant.
4. Add the spinach and cook for 3-4 minutes until wilted. Stir in the heavy cream and Parmesan cheese, cooking for an additional 2-3 minutes until the sauce thickens—season with salt and pepper to taste.
5. Slice the beef tenderloin and serve with the creamy spinach on the side.

Per serving:

Calories: 500 | Fats: 40g | Protein: 28g | Carbs: 3g | Net Carbs: 2g | Fiber: 1g
Fat 75% / Protein 23% / Carb 2%

MEATBALLS IN CREAMY PARMESAN SAUCE

Excellent

Medium

4 Servings

15 min.

25 min.

Ingredients:

For the Meatballs:
- 1 lb ground beef or pork
- 1/4 cup grated Parmesan cheese
- 1/4 cup almond flour
- 1 egg
- 1 teaspoon dried oregano
- 1 teaspoon garlic powder
- 1 teaspoon onion powder
- Salt and pepper to taste
- 2 tablespoons olive oil or butter

For the Creamy Parmesan Sauce:
- 1 cup heavy cream
- 1/2 cup grated Parmesan cheese
- 1 tablespoon butter
- 1 clove garlic, minced
- Salt and pepper to taste
- Fresh parsley for garnish (optional)

Instructions:

1. Mix ground meat, Parmesan, almond flour, egg, oregano, garlic powder, onion powder, salt, and pepper in a bowl. Shape into 12-14 meatballs.
2. Heat oil in a skillet over medium heat. Fry the meatballs for 6-8 minutes until browned and cooked through. Remove from the skillet.
3. Melt butter, garlic, and sauté in the same skillet for 30 seconds. Stir in cream and Parmesan, simmer for 2-3 minutes until thickened, and season with salt and pepper.
4. Add meatballs to the sauce and simmer for 2-3 minutes. Garnish with parsley and serve hot.

Per serving:

Calories: 400 | Fats: 34g | Protein: 20g | Carbs: 4g | Net Carbs: 3g | Fiber: 1g
Fat 80% / Protein 18% / Carb 2%

STUFFED BELL PEPPERS WITH MINCED MEAT, FETA CHEESE, AND TOMATOES

 Excellent   **Medium**   **2 Servings**   **15 min.**   **35 min.**

Ingredients:

- 2 large bell peppers, halved lengthwise and seeds removed
- 1/2 lb ground beef or pork
- 1/4 cup crumbled feta cheese
- 1/4 cup diced tomatoes (fresh or canned)
- 1/2 small onion, finely chopped

- 1 clove garlic, minced
- 1 tablespoon olive oil
- 1/2 teaspoon dried oregano
- 1/2 teaspoon dried basil
- Salt and pepper to taste
- Fresh parsley for garnish (optional)

Instructions:

1. Preheat the oven to 375°F (190°C).
2. Heat olive oil in a large skillet over medium heat. Add the chopped onion, garlic, and sauté until softened for 3-4 minutes. Add the ground beef (or pork) and cook for 8 minutes, breaking it apart until browned.
3. Stir in the diced tomatoes, oregano, basil, salt, and pepper. Cook for an additional 2-3 minutes until the flavors meld together. Remove from heat and mix in the crumbled feta cheese.
4. Stuff the halved bell peppers with the meat mixture, pressing it in neatly. Place the stuffed pepper halves in a baking dish.
5. Bake for 25-30 minutes or until the peppers are tender.
6. Remove from the oven, garnish with fresh parsley if desired, and serve hot.

Per serving:

Calories: 350 | Fats: 25g | Protein: 22g | Carbs: 8g | Net Carbs: 6g | Fiber: 2g
Fat 70% / Protein 25% / Carb 5%

Chapter 9
Veggies

Spinach: A Keto-Friendly Nutrient Boost

Spinach is a great choice on the keto diet, providing fiber, vitamins, and minerals with very few carbs. Loaded with vitamins A, C, and K, plus iron and magnesium, it supports immunity, bone health, and energy levels. Antioxidants in spinach also help reduce inflammation, making it a valuable addition to daily keto meals.

The fiber in spinach aids digestion and helps keep you full, which is essential for managing cravings. Its mild taste and versatility make it easy to use in various dishes, from salads to smoothies and stir-fries. Adding spinach regularly enriches your diet with essential nutrients while keeping carbs low.

CREAMED SPINACH SIDE DISH WITH ONION AND GARLIC

Excellent   **Easy**   **2 Servings**   **10 min.**   **15 min.**

Ingredients:

- 1/4 cup heavy cream
- 2 cloves garlic, minced
- 1/2 small onion, finely chopped
- 4 cups fresh spinach (about 8 oz)
- 1/4 cup cream cheese
- 2 tablespoons butter
- Salt and pepper to taste
- 1 tablespoon grated Parmesan cheese (optional)

Instructions:

1. Melt the butter in a large skillet over medium heat. Add the chopped onion, garlic, and sauté for 3-4 minutes until softened and fragrant.
2. Add the fresh spinach to the skillet and cook for 3-4 minutes until wilted.
3. Stir in the heavy cream and cream cheese, and cook for another 3-5 minutes, stirring constantly, until the mixture becomes creamy and thick.
4. Season with salt and pepper. Garnish with grated Parmesan cheese if desired, and serve immediately.

Per serving:

Calories: 280 | Fats: 24g | Protein: 6g | Carbs: 8g | Net Carbs: 4g | Fiber: 4g
Fat 82% / Protein 8% / Carb 10%

GARLICKY GREEN BEANS

Ingredients:

- 8 oz fresh green beans, trimmed
- 2 tablespoons butter
- 2 cloves garlic, minced
- Salt and pepper to taste
- 1 tablespoon lemon juice
- 1 tablespoon grated Parmesan cheese (optional)

Instructions:

1. Melt the butter in a large skillet over medium heat. Add the minced garlic and sauté for 30 seconds until fragrant.
2. Add the green beans to the skillet and sauté for 5-6 minutes, stirring occasionally, until the beans are tender but still crisp.
3. Season with salt, pepper, and optional lemon juice. Stir well to coat the green beans.
4. Remove from heat and sprinkle with Parmesan cheese if desired. Serve immediately.

Per serving:

Calories: 150 | Fats: 12g | Protein: 3g | Carbs: 8g | Net Carbs: 4g | Fiber: 4g
Fat 75% / Protein 8% / Carb 17%

Excellent   **2 Servings**

Medium   **5 min.**   **12 min.**

ZUCCHINI STIR-FRIED

Ingredients:

- 2 medium zucchini (about 10 oz each), cut into strips 5-6 cm long and 1-1.3 cm wide
- 2 tablespoons olive oil or butter
- 1/2 teaspoon chili flakes
- Salt and pepper to taste
- 1 tablespoon soy sauce or tamari (optional)
- 1 tablespoon sesame seeds (optional)
- 2 cloves garlic, minced

Instructions:

1. Heat the olive oil or butter in a large skillet over medium heat. Add the minced garlic and chili flakes (if used) and sauté for 30 seconds until fragrant.
2. Add the zucchini strips to the skillet and sauté for 7-10 minutes, stirring occasionally, until golden and tender.
3. Season with salt, pepper, and optional soy sauce or tamari. Stir well to coat the zucchini evenly.
4. Remove from heat, sprinkle with sesame seeds if desired, and serve immediately.

Per serving:

Calories: 400 | Fats: 32g | Protein: 22g | Carbs: 6g | Net Carbs: 4g | Fiber: 2g
Fat 75% / Protein 22% / Carb 3%

Broccoli: A Keto-Friendly Superfood

Broccoli is a top choice for the keto diet, offering fiber, vitamins, and minerals with very few carbs. Packed with vitamins C and K, along with folate and potassium, broccoli supports immunity, bone health, and overall vitality. Its antioxidant content also helps reduce inflammation, making it a great addition to a balanced keto diet.

High in fiber, broccoli aids digestion and keeps you feeling full, which is beneficial for managing cravings on keto. With a mild flavor and versatility, broccoli can be steamed, roasted, or added to stir-fries, enriching your meals with essential nutrients while keeping carbs low.

BAKED BROCCOLI IN A PAN WITH SESAME SEEDS

 Excellent   **Medium**   **2 Servings**   **10 min.**   **15 min.**

Ingredients:

- 1 medium head of broccoli (about 12 oz), cut into florets
- 2 tablespoons olive oil
- 1 tablespoon sesame seeds
- 1 tablespoon soy sauce (or tamari for gluten-free)
- 1 clove garlic, minced
- Salt and pepper to taste

Instructions:

1. Preheat your oven to 400°F (200°C). In a large bowl, toss the broccoli florets with olive oil, garlic, salt, and pepper.
2. Spread the broccoli evenly in a large oven-safe skillet or baking dish. Bake for 10-12 minutes until the broccoli starts to crisp.
3. Remove from the oven and drizzle with soy sauce. Sprinkle sesame seeds over the broccoli.
4. Return to the oven for 3-5 minutes until the sesame seeds are lightly toasted. Serve immediately.

Per serving:

Calories: 180 | Fats: 14g | Protein: 4g | Carbs: 9g | Net Carbs: 5g | Fiber: 4g
Fat 75% / Protein 9% / Carb 16%

CAULIFLOWER RICE WITH HERBS AND LEMON JUICE

Ingredients:

- 1 medium head of cauliflower, grated or processed into rice (about 2.5 cups)
- 2 tablespoons olive oil or butter

- 2 cloves garlic, minced
- 1/2 lemon (juice)
- 1/4 cup fresh parsley, chopped
- Salt and pepper to taste

Instructions:

1. Heat the olive oil or butter in a large skillet over medium heat. Add the minced garlic and sauté for about 30 seconds until fragrant.
2. Add the cauliflower rice to the skillet and sauté for 4-5 minutes until tender and lightly golden.
3. Remove from heat and stir in the lemon juice and chopped parsley—season with salt and pepper to taste.
4. Serve immediately, garnished with extra herbs if desired.

Per serving:

Calories: 150 | Fats: 12g | Protein: 2g | Carbs: 6g | Net Carbs: 3g | Fiber: 3g Fat 75% / Protein 2% / Carb 23%

Excellent

2 Servings

Medium

10 min.

10 min.

GREEN ASPARAGUS WITH HOLLANDAISE SAUCE

Ingredients:

- 1 medium head of cauliflower, grated or processed into rice (about 2.5 cups)
- 2 tablespoons olive oil or butter

- 2 cloves garlic, minced
- 1/2 lemon (juice)
- 1/4 cup fresh parsley, chopped
- Salt and pepper to taste

Instructions:

1. Heat olive oil in a large skillet over medium heat. Add minced garlic and sauté for 30 seconds until fragrant.
2. Add the asparagus, drizzle with lemon juice, and sauté for 2-3 minutes—season with salt and pepper. Cover and cook for another 2-3 minutes until tender.
3. Melt the butter for the sauce. Whisk together egg yolks, lemon juice, and Dijon mustard in a bowl. Gradually whisk in the melted butter until thickened.
4. Serve the asparagus topped with hollandaise sauce.

Per serving:

Calories: 310 | Fats: 28g | Protein: 6g | Carbs: 6g | Net Carbs: 3g | Fiber: 3g Fat 80% / Protein 8% / Carb 12%

CAULIFLOWER PUREE WITH CREAM

Ingredients:

- 1 medium head of cauliflower (about 12 oz), chopped into florets
- 1/4 cup heavy cream
- 2 tablespoons butter
- 1 clove garlic, minced (optional)
- Salt and pepper to taste
- 1 tablespoon grated Parmesan cheese (optional)

Instructions:

1. Steam or boil the cauliflower florets for 8-10 minutes until tender. Drain well.
2. Melt the butter in a large pot over medium heat. Add the garlic (if using) and sauté for 30 seconds until fragrant.
3. Add the cooked cauliflower, heavy cream, salt, and pepper to the pot. Use a blender or immersion blender to puree the mixture until smooth and creamy.
4. Adjust seasoning to taste, and sprinkle with Parmesan cheese if desired. Serve hot.

Per serving:

Calories: 200 | Fats: 18g | Protein: 4g | Carbs: 7g | Net Carbs: 4g | Fiber: 3g
Fat 85% / Protein 8% / Carb 7%

Excellent   **2 Servings**

Medium   **10 min.**   **10 min.**

ZUCCHINI PASTA TOPPED WITH TOMATOES AND BASIL PESTO

Ingredients:

- 2 medium zucchinis, cut into long spaghetti-like strips
- 1/4 cup basil pesto (store-bought or homemade)
- 1/2 cup cherry tomatoes, halved

Instructions:

1. Heat 1 tablespoon of olive oil in a large skillet over medium heat. Add the zucchini strips and sauté for 5-6 minutes until tender but still firm—season with salt and pepper.
2. Remove the zucchini noodles from the skillet and place on serving plates.
3. Heat the remaining 1 tablespoon of olive oil in the same skillet and quickly sauté the cherry tomatoes for 2-3 minutes until they are slightly soft.
4. Top the zucchini strips with basil pesto and sautéed tomatoes. If desired, garnish with fresh basil leaves. Serve immediately.

Per serving:

Calories: 450 | Fats: 35g | Protein: 30g | Carbs: 4g | Net Carbs: 2g | Fiber: 2g
Fat 75% / Protein 25% / Carb 5%

Chapter 10.
Conclusion: Embracing Your Keto Journey

Reflecting on Your Progress

As you reach the conclusion of this book, take a moment to look back at the remarkable journey you've undertaken. Transitioning to the keto lifestyle is an achievement in itself—one that requires commitment, learning, and adaptation. By now, you've developed a deep understanding of how the ketogenic diet can transform your life and bring lasting health benefits.

From shedding unwanted weight to experiencing improved mental clarity, stable energy levels, and better metabolic health, keto offers a sustainable, science-backed approach to enhanced wellness. This journey isn't merely about dietary changes; it's about embracing a lifestyle that aligns with your health goals and sets a foundation for long-term vitality.

Mastering the Basics for Long-term Success

The fundamentals you've acquired throughout this book—from balancing macronutrients to understanding ketosis—are powerful tools that will continue to support you long after you finish reading. With this guidance, you can confidently plan meals, avoid common pitfalls, and make smart, keto-friendly choices even in challenging situations.

These foundational skills are invaluable for long-term success, providing the confidence to sustain the diet and make keto a permanent part of your lifestyle. With each meal you prepare and each choice you make, you are building a solid framework for maintaining your health and enjoying the profound benefits of keto for years to come.

Keeping a Balanced and Flexible Approach

Keto isn't just a diet; it's a dynamic lifestyle that evolves with you. Flexibility and patience are crucial to making keto a natural and enjoyable part of your life. There may be days when sticking to keto feels challenging, and that's perfectly normal. Remember, keto is adaptable to your lifestyle—allowing room for adjustments, experimentation, and personal growth.

The more you incorporate variety into your meals and explore new recipes, the more fulfilling your keto experience will be. A balanced approach keeps the diet sustainable, allowing you to enjoy your journey without feeling restricted.

Staying Inspired on Your Keto Path

Maintaining motivation is essential for long-term success. Keto offers endless opportunities for culinary exploration, so continue to set achievable goals, discover new recipes, and celebrate the progress you make along the way. Dedication and creativity will be your greatest allies, turning keto from a dietary choice into an enjoyable and enriching lifestyle.

Challenge yourself to experiment with different ingredients, try new cooking techniques, and take pride in the positive changes you bring to your health and well-being. Keto is a rewarding path, but like any worthwhile endeavor, it requires resilience and an open mind.

Your New Keto Lifestyle

Congratulations on taking this meaningful step toward a healthier, more energetic you! As you incorporate keto into your everyday routine, remember that this lifestyle is about balance, joy, and commitment to your wellness.

Each choice you make, each meal you prepare, and each goal you achieve contributes to a stronger, healthier future. Keto is not about perfection; it's about progress, self-care, and a dedication to long-term health. Embrace this journey, knowing that every effort is an investment in yourself, creating a foundation for years of vibrant health.

Thank you for choosing this journey!

If you enjoyed this book, we would love to hear your thoughts in an Amazon review. Your feedback helps others discover the benefits of the keto lifestyle. Don't forget to join the author's reader club to stay connected, share your experiences, and gain access to exclusive content. Let's continue the journey toward a healthier, more balanced life!

APPENDIX
Conversion Tables

Here are some common measurements used in cooking and their conversions into other systems of measure.

Measurement Conversions

Measurement	Imperial	Metric
1 teaspoon	1/6 fl oz	5 mL
1 tablespoon	1/2 fl oz	15 mL
1 fluid ounce	1/8 cup	30 mL
1 cup	8 fl oz	240 mL
1 pint	16 fl oz	480 mL
1 quart	32 fl oz	960 mL
1 gallon	128 fl oz	3.8 L

Temperature Conversions

Fahrenheit (°F)	Celsius (°C)
250	121
300	149
350	177
400	204
450	232
500	260

Weight Conversions

Imperial	Metric
1 ounce	28 grams
2 ounces	56 grams
4 ounces	113 grams
1 pound	454 grams
2 pounds	907 grams

Meaning of icons

Icon	Meaning
	Good, Great, Excellent
	Serves for Persons
	Easy, Medium, Difficult
	Preparation Time
	Cooking Time

For notes

Made in the USA
Monee, IL
13 March 2025

13963560R00046